A LOVELY PLACE, A FIGHTING PLACE, A CHARMER:

The Baltimore Anthology

MORE CITY ANTHOLOGIES FROM BELT

The Indianapolis Anthology

The Dayton Anthology

The Louisville Anthology

The Gary Anthology

Car Bombs to Cookie Tables: The Youngstown Anthology, Second Edition

The Columbus Anthology

The St. Louis Anthology

Under Purple Skies: The Minneapolis Anthology

The Milwaukee Anthology

Rust Belt Chicago: An Anthology

Grand Rapids Grassroots: An Anthology

Happy Anyway: A Flint Anthology

The Akron Anthology

Right Here, Right Now: The Buffalo Anthology

The Cleveland Anthology, Second Edition

The Pittsburgh Anthology

A Detroit Anthology

The Cincinnati Anthology

06-30-22

for shawn
all the
best
rahul

A LOVELY PLACE,
A FIGHTING PLACE,
A CHARMER:

The Baltimore Anthology

Belt Publishing

First Edition 2022
ISBN: 978-1-953368-26-3

Belt Publishing
5322 Fleet Avenue, Cleveland, OH 44105
www.beltpublishing.com

Book design by Meredith Pangrace
Cover by David Wilson

CONTENTS

CONTENTS

Introduction

RAFAEL ALVAREZ

So, you think you know Baltimore because you own a TV?

Then you must suffer from a chronic condition known here in Crabtown as ARD: Ain't Right Disorder!

In 1987, when hometown boy John Waters was filming *Hairspray* here, he cast Pia Zadora as a "hippie chick" living in squalor with a hippie boyfriend who was played by the late rock star Ric Ocasek.

Looking around at the boarded-up buildings, abandoned vehicles, and trash—a slice of sad-ass iconography that would become synonymous with Baltimore via HBO's *The Wire*—Zadora complimented Waters on the authenticity of the set.

"Pia," a bemused Waters is said to have replied, "this isn't a set. People *live* here."

This book introduces you to those people: ice-house laborers, civil rights leaders in Congress and on the street, poets impersonating physicians, horseradish kings, and Hall of Fame ballplayers. All the while giving the lie that Baltimore is synonymous with anything but people making it from one day to the next.

Baltimoreans are often strange (Abe Sherman, the city's most famous newsstand vendor, threw almost as many people out of his shop as he served) and more often indefatigable. You will find fact and fiction in this book, some of it delivered in verse celebrating a town where the phrase, "She's a character," is taken as a compliment.

In the late nineteenth century, the work of Edgar Allan Poe—who is buried here at the corner of Fayette and Greene Streets—was forbidden in the childhood home of a privileged New Yorker named Edith Wharton.

The snooty elders of the future author of *The House of Mirth* reportedly denigrated the great poet as the "drunken and demoralized Baltimorean."

Just the type of mug that a local bus driver, line cook, or stevedore would welcome as "my kind of guy."

When I exiled myself from Baltimore for five years to pan for fool's gold in Tinseltown, I was often asked what my hometown was *really* like.

"You know all those great John Waters movies? *Hairspray*? *Crybaby*?" I'd say, "They're documentaries."

The waters along the edge of this colonial port city—where bolt holes for shackles that detained slaves sold at auction can still be found—are deep enough to supply material for a dozen volumes about life in the Queen City of the Patapsco River.

No one featured in this book is more important than those who were left out, among them West Baltimorean entertainer Cab Calloway, who put the word "boogie" into common usage; Theodore "Balls" Maggio, who skimmed the harbor for lost balls and then sold them back to kids on the street; Thurgood Marshall, the first Black Supreme Court justice; and a Pimlico racetrack balloon salesman named Mr. Diz.

We wish there could have been more, particularly since the city of Mencken and Lucille Clifton is rich in writers who would do them justice. But as my late Polish grandmother—a true East Baltimore "hon," as in *"Whatcha doin' hon?"*—often said, "You can't put ten pounds of *gówno* into a five-pound bag."

So this is what we shook out, straight from the Land of Pleasant Living where people still sit on their front steps to drink beer no longer brewed here; take two buses to work three jobs; and swear they're never coming into the city again because "it's really getting bad" (a rant heard since the 1960s) while others declare they'll never leave.

Over the years, I have given many talks to young people who believe they want to become writers. Without fail, a kid will raise their hand and ask: "Where do you get your ideas?"

"You live in Baltimore," I tell them. "Have you walked outside today?"

The author with his Baltimore journal. Credit: Jennifer Bishop.

Reporter / Reverend / Baltimorean

M. DION THOMPSON

Baltimore baffled me at first. In some ways, after thirty years of living here, it still does. What to make of its head-spinning contrasts in neighborhoods? Of its story and its dual memory of itself? I say dual because all you would have to do is lay 1950s issues of the *Baltimore Sun* or the *News-American* side by side with *Afro-American* and you would see two different worlds. One white, one Black—each giving only the faintest hint that the other exists.

As I said, this baffled me at first. Even more so was a drive through town on an early visit to find a place to live. Our driver, a future colleague of mine at the aforementioned *Sun*, took us all over Baltimore, giving bits of information about the neighborhoods and the city I would soon call home and be writing about.

What I most remember was the warning given as we drove through Hampden: You don't want to live here. They don't like Blacks.

Huh? It was the last two years of the 1980s, and I was being warned against moving into a certain neighborhood. I don't know if I was more disturbed that Hampden was off-limits or that this fact was an accepted piece of the city's life. We did not move into Hampden. But a year or so later, a Black family did. Their claims of being Moorish fooled no one. And they were gone within a week or two. All I could do was shake my head and say to myself, "I guess it's true."

That was more than a generation ago, and I use it as a marker of how the city was when I arrived and what it has become. Today, "the Avenue" in Hampden is hip. Hon Fest is a Baltimore party, complete with beehive hairdos and cat-eye glasses. Pink Flamingos—honoring the John Waters film of the same name—are one of the city's emblems along with Natty Boh and the cartoon Oriole baseball bird.

A neighbor of mine once had a T-shirt with the familiar National Bohemian "one-eyed little man" character on the front, but this one sported an afro do. Who was he? Natty Bro', of course.

I am baffled and amused. Not only do we have "The Night of 1,000 Elvises" but a Black Elvis too. I interviewed him once, the self-proclaimed high priest of all things Elvi.

And I am pained by the history that comes with the territory.

If Maryland is said to be "America in miniature," then Baltimore can equally lay claim. All of our country's history is here. Streets such as Paca and Howard bear the names of Revolutionary War heroes. Walk along Pratt Street and you're walking where slaves were held before being marched in chains to Fell's Point. From there they were loaded onto ships headed for the auction blocks of New Orleans.

Somewhere between the old President Street Station—so named because Lincoln passed through on the way to his first inauguration—and the original city neighborhood of Fells Point is where Frederick Douglass caught a train and escaped to freedom. The alley street where he built a church—South Dallas Street—is also known as Douglass Row.

Baltimore gave the country its trains and clipper ships, Edgar Allan Poe and Babe Ruth, Frank Zappa, Chick Webb and Billie Holiday, Thurgood Marshall, Barbara Mikulski, and Nancy Pelosi.

Dual histories abound. Yet, what is history? Is it a tale told by winners, a selective concoction of fact and fiction, half-truths and dreams seen through rose-colored glasses? Is it a feel-good celebration, or a catalog of wrongs? Or is it simply the ground on which we stand?

As always, the city is changing, and yet Baltimore wears its history in its neighborhoods: Sandtown, Greektown, Little Italy, Druid Hill, and Pigtown. These are real and distinct places—stubborn, defiant in their fierce grip on identity even when those identities no longer ring true.

I, for one, will not stop calling the stretch along Washington Boulevard, "Pigtown." Developers and realtors prefer "Washington Village" to the original name—given when pigs in route to slaughter ran the streets—but in the past forty years, the more genteel name has never taken hold.

And I pray it never does. The loss would be too great. It would feel like an erasure. What's in a name, you ask? Plenty.

Many years ago, an assignment took me to the far end of Boston Street in Canton. I don't remember the story. What I do remember is noticing the street was being torn up and repaved. What's going on? I wondered. There was nothing but empty warehouses lining an uneven street riven with twisted and broken railroad tracks.

How was I to know that Canton would become the "gold coast" of marinas and gentrification? That "Mister Boh" would be flashing a neon smile up on Brewer's Hill and that those old warehouses would be turned into condominiums with waterfront views?

I left town for three years in the early 2000s to attend seminary in New York City. When I returned, a vacant plot of land between downtown and Fell's Point had been transformed into a little bit of New York City and christened "Harbor East." That was just the beginning. Condos, townhouses, and apartment towers line the harbor rim from Canton to Fort McHenry.

The "Golden L"—a pattern in a map of the city where the "haves" tend to live and the "have nots" do not—is in full effect. And therein lies our challenge. How do we bring everyone along?

The uprising after Freddie Gray's death in 2015 told us there is much work to do. Greenmount Avenue between Thirty-Ninth Street and Cold Spring Lane on the north side can't be the dividing line of separate worlds forever. The beat-up neighborhood around Edmondson Avenue and Carey Street can't continue its decline, out of sight and out of mind as all eyes turn to the glitter that attracts tourists and out-of-towners who can't believe how relatively inexpensive real estate remains here compared to Washington just down the road.

Baltimore's work is America's work. We've pulled down our Confederate statues and watched as protestors toppled the Christopher Columbus statue in Little Italy and rolled it into the Inner Harbor.

The aftermath of George Floyd's death beneath the knee of a Minneapolis police officer finds us with the same urgent need to reimagine ourselves and our possibilities, to reconcile our past with our present and move into a better future. Emphasis on the "our." Though our circumstances may differ, we are all in this together. It is no use pretending otherwise.

Progress will be incremental, but we will progress. It's a law of nature and of Baltimore. It will happen in ways that may startle us at first, but then, over time, it will become part of the fabric of life in Charm City.

The other evening, I was walking home in Bolton Hill near the historic Maryland Institute College of Art and heard a jazz band playing. The snap of drums, the moody tones of an electric keyboard, and the smooth, "round" sound of a trumpet filled the air. At first, I thought Brown Memorial Presbyterian Church might be having a free concert, but the church doors were closed.

It turned out a group of young Black men were giving a "pop-up" concert in the 1300 block of Park Avenue. The crowd was mixed in age and color, all grooving at an appropriate social distance. Many wore masks, de rigueur in the pandemic of 2020.

This wasn't the Bolton Hill of thirty years ago, or even one hundred years ago, when the newly formed Mount Royal Improvement Association could proudly boast that the neighborhood was a "protected area" and that "the greatest achievement of the Mount Royal Improvement Association has been the subjecting of the property in the area to restrictions to white occupancy only."

This was the Bolton Hill of now, a snapshot of Baltimore slowly getting comfortable with itself.

Elijah Cummings: Statesman from the West Side, 1951–2019

JOHN SARBANES

The Elijah Cummings I knew was a prince of a human being. He possessed a combination of wisdom and soul that touched those around him and made them better equipped for life's journey.

I remember sitting with him in the House of Representatives, talking about Baltimore, the city he loved, and the people of his district for whom he cared deeply. He had a special place in his heart for young people, particularly those facing challenges and obstacles, because he saw himself in them and knew that if he could overcome so much, then so could they.

Sometimes, when we talked about how he rose to serve as chairman of the powerful House Committee on Oversight and Reform, it was clear that he was amazed and humbled at the trajectory of his own life.

Elijah had favorite sayings:

"We are better than that!"

"Our children are the messages we send to a future we will never see."

"We must fight for the soul of our democracy."

He would greet every audience with "Good morning," and if the response was tepid, he would scold: "Come on, we can do better than that. GOOD MORNING!" And the room would come alive.

These were his exhortations to the multitudes, but the most moving and motivating interactions I witnessed were when Elijah was talking one-on-one to the people who sought him out. He wasn't passing time. He wasn't checking a box. He really, truly wanted to know everything about you and, most importantly, if you were you realizing your dreams, if you were moving forward.

And I never saw him leave one of those conversations without saying simply, "How can I help?"

He had a wonderful laugh—deep, resonant, playful, and absolutely infectious. When Elijah laughed, you couldn't help laughing along. Somehow, he had figured out how to balance the crushing pressure of his work with the small, beautifully human moments that he found in life's daily interactions.

US Congressman Elijah Cummings. Credit: J. M. Giordano.

Why do we miss him so much? I can't speak for others, but his voice—that amazing voice which could thunder one minute and whisper the next—made me feel safe. It made me feel hopeful that I—we—could make it through to the other side of the storm.

When, in his last days, he became weaker, the voice was still there, still powerful, still demanding of the world that we do more for those with less. But it was also reflective and always humble. At times, Elijah was unsure about the contribution he had made. At one of the last public events that we did together, he wondered out loud whether people would remember him as someone who had made a difference. We know the answer.

He is gone now. But his voice still rings in our ears, giving us courage to carry on, to finish the job, to win the fight. Thank you, Elijah, for the opportunity to know you.

Charm City

LYNNE VITI

Downtown disappeared as we packed up our childhood things, went to
college, resisted the pull of home,
succumbed to the scent of independence.
We didn't know about birth control, weren't ready for sex,

spent hours gazing at fashion photos of formal dresses
for proms or military balls at the southern men's schools. We borrowed
long white gloves, clutch bags, fake pearls, monitored our alcohol intake,
fended off advances,

watched foreign films with subtitles, learned to roll joints. Uptown, we
practiced our driving, took our road tests.
City buses were for others—we were meant for better things. Downtown,
the department stores packed up, moved to the suburbs.

The posh steakhouses grew tired and empty as their patrons died off, got
too old to travel, began to lose their teeth.
The shoppers' favorite drugstore closed the counter service—where we
lunched on tuna sandwiches, chips on the side—

The management evaded those sit-ins by students—undergrads of
different races in chinos and V-neck sweaters. Secretaries and file clerks
tottering in heels across cobblestones, over trolley tracks, leather bags in
hand, once ubiquitous,

disembarking from city buses each morning—
vanished almost overnight, along with the appellation "Miss." The boy we
celebrated because he could drink a case of beer
—and not pass out—was drafted into the 5th Infantry, C Company,

died in Quang Tri Province, the memory of his round face,
his Beatle haircut, so faint now. We traced his name on the Wall.
Downtown, the cranes went to work making a shiny marketplace in the
footprint of the old harbor. The spice factory migrated

to the county, dispersed cinnamon air among cul-de-sacs. Shops and row houses burned, were abandoned, boarded up.

Then the hometown football team sneaked out of town at midnight, the moving vans heading west to the city of Indians.

There is beauty here if only you look for it . . . Credit: Macon Street Books.

East Federal Street

RON CASSIE

Monica Bland missed her turn in the ashen light. Driving through one of Baltimore's hanging-by-a-thread, mixed-use neighborhoods (abandoned warehouses, crumbling row homes, shuttered churches), she was picking up her two godchildren from their Saturday 4-H youth meeting.

"Absent-minded, daydreaming," she said. "Maybe I was tired."

Veering from her normal route, Bland suddenly found herself, through the mist and fog, staring up at a gray, photorealistic mural on the side of a two-story concrete wall. It was a painting recreated from a 1956 black-and-white photograph in the *Afro-American* newspaper that she'd never seen: a proud father and mother, well-dressed and happy, with seven of their smiling kids strung from tallest to shortest. The family is seen walking together down a city sidewalk next to spit-polished Madison Square.

Each child—from the teenage girl, who is nearly as tall as her dad, to the youngest—carries brown-paper wrapped boxes. They'd been shopping for Easter shoes.

"And I realized, as the faces in the mural are looking back at me, that I know this family," recalls Bland, still in disbelief, months later in a midtown coffee shop. "It's my grandparents, all my aunts, my uncle, and my mother."

Artist Michael Owen, of Baltimore Love Project renown, had painted the larger-than-life image as it appeared in the paper on Holy Saturday, March 30, 1956. The effort was a collaboration with local photographer Webster Phillips, whose grandfather, Henry Phillips (father of longtime *Baltimore Sun* photographer Irv Phillips), shot the original for the *Afro-American*.

A plaque next to the mural asked viewers to contact the younger Phillips if they could ID the people featured: "Help us save Baltimore history."

Startled and moved, Bland dialed the number.

"I was blown away," Phillips says. "You hope you get a call like that. You don't really expect it."

Walter Dean Sr., the father in the tie and glasses in the photo and Bland's grandfather, raised those seven children—plus two older brothers already out of the house by the time the picture was taken—on a postal worker's salary.

"Can you imagine?" Bland sighs. Her grandmother, Ruth, a stay-at-home mom until the last of the kids started school, supplemented the household as a nursing assistant at the long-since-closed Lutheran Hospital.

The image remains a striking portrait of an upwardly mobile Black family two years after *Brown v. Board of Education* in segregated Baltimore.

"Everyone in that photo made it to the middle class," says the fifty-four-year-old Bland, who runs a small educational business. "It was the next generation, including me, that began experiencing trauma and problems as the city, and life, began falling apart in the seventies and eighties."

Bland attempted suicide as a young, single mother of a two-year-old. She would later lose her older brother to mental health issues and substance abuse, not learning until years after the fact that he'd been buried as a John Doe in San Diego. Following that heartbreak, her youngest brother was shot and killed in 2008 in a street in Northeast Baltimore, not far from the Pimlico racetrack.

Bland's paternal family came to Baltimore from the same Church Creek area on the Eastern Shore of Maryland as Harriet Tubman, about six miles outside Cambridge. It was her great-grandfather, William Dean, who had been the first to migrate to the city shortly after the turn of the twentieth century.

He fled the grinding rural poverty of his upbringing as a single man in his twenties, like so many others during the Great Migration, seeking work and relief from the oppressive Deep South culture on the other side of the Chesapeake Bay.

Throughout the 1960s, what were then known as "race riots" swept the nation. Most, like the violence in Baltimore, began after the murder of the Rev. Martin Luther King Jr. in 1968. Order unraveled earlier in Cambridge—in 1963 and again in 1967.

As a girl, Bland returned often to the Eastern Shore with her parents, grandparents, aunts, uncles, and cousins for annual visits over the Memorial Day weekend. She recalls the country cookouts, church on those hot summer Sundays, and most of all, stopping at Dairy Queen on the round trip back to the city.

Her great-grandfather had been born on the Eastern Shore in the first generation after the Civil War, dying just three years before Bland was born. He eventually landed a job with union wages and benefits in Baltimore at what would become the world's biggest steel mill at Sparrows Point, setting his family on firm economic ground. He retired there with a good pension and health care.

Bland's mother, Sonia, and her grandparents and eight siblings were one of the first families to move from East Baltimore to the new Cherry Hill development in far south Baltimore in the mid-1940s.

It was the first suburban-style planned community for African Americans in the United States, built to handle the massive influx of World War II defense industry workers into Baltimore. It was also probably the most obvious example of residential segregation by design ever in the country.

After years of delays because of white backlash at other proposed sites, Cherry Hill went up quickly once the federal government demanded Baltimore address its shortage of acceptable housing for African Americans. Aspirational Black families rushed into the sparkling row houses and apartment buildings even before a school, shopping center, or grocery store went up. Infrastructure, including a generous park and community center, soon followed.

"It was a place where the schools were bright and clean and people who grew up there went to work and found good jobs, years later, at BGE, the Social Security Administration, and the phone company," says Linda Morris, who is from the neighborhood and is the author of *Cherry Hill: Raising Successful Black Children in Jim Crow Baltimore.*

"You know that African proverb, 'It takes a village to raise a child?'" Bland says. "That was Cherry Hill."

One of Bland's aunts built a career as a Social Security administrator. Another aunt became a hospital administrator. Her mother ultimately rose from bank teller to branch manager.

Her uncle, Walter Dean Jr., was among the leaders of the Read's Drugstore sit-ins and Northwood Shopping Center segregation protests while he was a student at what was then Morgan State College. He later served in the Air Force, taught urban affairs at Baltimore City Community College, and was elected to Maryland's general assembly.

"You know what is amazing?" Bland says. "I've lost two of my brothers, but my mother and everyone in that mural, other than my grandparents, who have passed, is alive and healthy."

————————

The short answer in white circles to the question, "What happened to Baltimore?" is often reactionary and flippant—"the riots," the April 1968 crisis following Rev. Martin Luther King's assassination in Memphis.

In truth, the city's population had peaked eighteen years prior and was already in decline. But it's also not a wrong answer. White retail businesses and residents—and Black, middle-class residents, too—decamped over the city line to the counties in huge numbers in the seventies, eighties, and nineties, with much of the city's tax base and jobs in tow. Most moved to Baltimore County along with Harford, Anne Arundel, and to a lesser degree, Carroll County.

The riots, however, did not create the problems in the city's hypersegregated Black neighborhoods in East and West Baltimore.

The four nights of looting and burning in 1968 were the capstone of decades of these kinds of racially discriminatory policies and practices, the most notorious of which was actually passed by the city council in 1910, just as Bland's great-grandfather and the first Great Migration wave was arriving.

The *Baltimore Sun* called it "The Negro Invasion." That landmark, discriminatory housing ordinance, eventually cast down by the Supreme Court, forbade white homeowners on majority-white blocks from selling to Black buyers and vice versa. But other discriminatory policies and practices over the decades ensued, as chronicled in the groundbreaking book *Not in My Neighborhood: How Bigotry Shaped a Great American City* by Antero Pietila.

Those included, but were not limited to, blockbusting and redlining by the Federal Housing Administration, which literally mapped red lines around Black neighborhoods and were intended to discourage loans. Similarly, GI Bill benefits, which included not just tuition dollars but job training funding and business and home loans, too, were distributed with shocking discrimination in Baltimore.

The city's increasingly Black public school system suffered from underfunding year after year, and then eventually the so-called War on Drugs was launched in the city's poorest neighborhoods, incarcerating tens of thousands of Black youths and young men.

The country's sixth-largest city in the 1950, imbued with the ethics of productivity and the American Dream, has since been effectively disassembled, losing more than 100,000 manufacturing jobs between 1950 and 1995.

One-third of Baltimore's population has left, leaving a dystopian 17,000 vacant homes and buildings in their wake. None of this shows any sign of reversing, as violent crime and murder continues to rise at the highest rates in the city's history.

Another sign of the times? In 2015, a one-million-square-foot Amazon fulfillment center sprang up on the site of a demolished General Motors plant that had once employed 7,000 United Auto Workers. Three years later, at Sparrows Point—atop the similarly demolished grounds where Bland's great-grandfather, like thousands of other blue-collar Black workers, found a home—a second, 855,000-square-foot Amazon fulfillment center popped up.

The thousands of packaging jobs at Amazon, the highest-valued company in the world owned by the wealthiest man in the world, pay half the wages of a union steel or automobile job. And they don't include the health, pension, vacation, sick, and family leave benefits, nor the job protections that typically come with a collective bargaining agreement.

"As a child, I remember growing up in the 1970s as a good period—mothers scrubbing their front stoops, playing with friends in the park," Bland says. "In reality, looking back as an adult, my mother was a single mom, and all my friends were growing up in single-parent homes.

"The loss of those good jobs, the economic impact on families, was already taking its toll. Where were the men supposed to go to work? It just wasn't as apparent as it would become. But it didn't just happen. It was caused. Segregation and political decisions did this."

It seems like a crazy coincidence, but in Baltimore, family histories run through all kinds of history.

Back in 2015, Bland managed the Hallmark card section at the CVS that was looted and set afire on national television during the uprising. Her daughter, a member of the National Guard, was working off-duty security at Camden Yards the same night—when the Orioles game was canceled because of the rioting.

"After everything died down at the game, I had to walk home because none of the buses, nothing, was moving downtown," guardswoman Katrina Bland recounts. "I started walking in one direction and saw a car burning. I turned down another street and saw a truck on fire. I went another way and saw people breaking into a store and running out with stuff. It was surreal, and I felt like I was being funneled toward that CVS at Penn-North.

"I texted my mother to let her know I was okay, but I could smell the smoke from the CVS before I got there."

Noted her mother: "And yet how do you explain this to people who don't know Baltimore? I love this city through everything. There are so many good people here. I don't want to live anywhere else."

Bland herself had left school at nineteen after learning she was pregnant. She eventually got therapy to deal with her depression. She turned to her church and gardening for healing, becoming a certified master gardener.

She returned to college and earned an associate's degree in education, subsequently homeschooling her four children rather than sending them across an increasingly chaotic city to an increasingly chaotic public school system. Her youngest daughter recently graduated from the University of Iowa, her son is an aspiring artist in the city, and her other daughter is a social worker.

Bland's children prove the city isn't without hope, but Bland knows how tough the rows are to plow in wide swaths of Baltimore.

"There are parts of the city that are doing great, but we all know there are two Baltimores. It's the haves and have-nots," she said.

One gets investment, tax breaks, and their trash collected; schools and recreation centers close in the other.

"Children are like seeds. No matter how good the seed may be, it won't bud and bloom if it isn't planted in good soil, watered, and cared for," said Bland, recalling her grandmother's love of roses. "The soil in Baltimore isn't fertile like it once was."

In the Moonlight

ASHLEY MINNER

My Aunt Jeanette—born a Locklear—arrived in Baltimore City for the first time as a teenager, in 1957. She says the water tasted terrible and the people were eating bugs. Of course, what looked like bugs to her were really steamed crabs, which she had never seen while growing up in rural Robeson County.

She says, "When I first come to Baltimore, I saw all those tall buildings. Now, I come from a house with just three rooms. When I got to the city and saw those buildings, I didn't like it. I wanted to go home. I wanted to go back to North Carolina."

It was summer vacation, and she had come to visit her older sister, Bonnie, who was living in a three-bedroom, second-floor apartment on East Baltimore Street, across from Sid's Ranch House, with her husband and their four kids. "It was . . . togetherness," she remembers, with a smile.

Life in Baltimore was exciting, too. "We'd be sitting out on the steps in the evenings. You just didn't want to miss anything. That was the social thing to do, sit on the steps and talk to your neighbors."

As time went by, more and more neighbors looked and sounded familiar—not because Aunt Jeanette was getting used to Baltimore, but because so many were arriving from back home, seeking work in the city.

"Home," to Lumbee Indians, is approximately four hundred miles due south of here. It is a land of pine trees and fields, with swamps at the edges and a river running through. The people there share a distinct accent, unique in all the world. They descend from a diverse group of ancestors who fled disease, enslavement, and colonial warfare to coalesce in Robeson County, well before the founding of the United States.

Though they run the full gamut of skin colors, eye colors, hair colors, and hair textures, they recognize each other upon sight—even, and especially, away from "home." They know each other through vast webs of extended kinship. The average Lumbee can rattle off generations of family names from multiple branches, easily identifying connections. One of the first things one "Lum" will ask another is "Who's your people?"

At "home," church is an integral part of life, and singing is everywhere. It is soulful, artful. It actually gets dark at night there because it's in the country. Even in town, everything shuts down early.

In the time Aunt Jeanette came to Baltimore, it was still the Jim Crow South, where Americans from other regions are always surprised to learn there was triracial segregation. Imagine three separate school systems—Black, White, and Indian. Imagine three different sections in the movie theater.

Also, during this time, many Lumbee families found themselves subsisting as sharecroppers on their homeland. They recall this as a modern-day form of slavery and cite is as the primary impetus for migration north.

Many got jobs in factories, like General Motors; Crown, Cork, and Seal; Western Electric; or Life-Like Products. Others took to trades like drywall, roofing, brick masonry, and painting.

Cousins sent for cousins, children for parents, sisters for brothers, and on and on until so many had settled around East Baltimore and Ann Streets that people started to call the area "the reservation." The block where Aunt Jeanette first stayed—the 1700 block of East Baltimore Street—was at the heart of it. And "down on the corner was the Moonlight where everybody hung out."

The Moonlight at 1 North Broadway was a twenty-four-hour, Greek-owned diner with a liquor license.

The food was cheap and good, and no one seemed to mind when patrons ordered a cup of coffee and then stayed for hours. It actually *was* where everyone hung out then—not just Indians but everyone in the neighborhood—which has perhaps always been in transition.

It was home to German and Irish immigrants in the mid-nineteenth century. Around the turn of the century, it became primarily Jewish. Later, it was Polish, with "Polish Wall Street"— more than a few Polish banking establishments—only a few blocks away.

In the postwar years, when literally thousands of Lumbee Indians appeared on the scene, the city reacted in various ways. Baltimore was understood then, as it is now, to be Black and White. Folks weren't quite sure what to make of this new population that identified as neither.

Southeastern district police officers sometimes jokingly called the Lumbees "Lombardees," due to their proximity to Lombard Street. Police assigned to "the reservation" called themselves "Indian Fighters." Westerns were all the rage at the time.

On Saturday nights, teenagers of the neighborhood visited the McKim School-turned community center—a magnificent, Parthenon-esque structure up on the 1100 block of East Baltimore Street near Central Avenue—for social dances. Aunt Jeanette says for Lumbee kids, too, "that was the place to be."

"What were they were dancing to?" I asked.

(2109 Lamley Street), and a gas station, now a 7-Eleven, at the corner of Broadway and Lombard Street.

In the "frequented" category, there were several more restaurants, a deli, pharmacies, and many bars, including the (infamous) Volcano (31 North Ann Street), Sid's Ranch House Tavern (1741 East Baltimore Street), Vince's (6 North Wolfe Street), New Jazz City (1829 East Pratt Street), and Sadie's (624 South Broadway). There was also a pool hall (1725 East Baltimore Street).

An American Indian community center—211 South Broadway then; 113 South Broadway today—would soon be in the works, with much of the planning taking place at the Moonlight, stretched out over some of those single-cup-of-coffee-hours-long stints.

"The Greeks and the Indians got along really good. Maybe because the Greeks made good food," Aunt Jeanette says, laughing.

Though she ate for free at the Moonlight whenever she worked, Aunt Jeanette also faced all of the perils of being a young female waitress. When she had had enough, she quit and walked herself down to the vinegar works, at the foot of Broadway on the corner of Thames Street.

She told the manager, "I need you to give me a job or support me and my baby." He laughed and she got a job.

In time, Aunt Jeanette moved a few miles east from the reservation to Greektown and enrolled her daughter in elementary school there. She would eventually settle even further southeast, in Dundalk, where, some sixty years later, most of Baltimore's Lumbee Indians would be living and where she still lives today. She has since retired from her last job—director, Indian Education Program, Baltimore City Public Schools.

The reservation started to break up around the same time that the Moonlight closed in 1972.

Indians who were able to move—like Aunt Jeanette—did. The desire for something better was accelerated when the city of Baltimore enacted an urban renewal plan that demolished many of the homes and businesses that made up "the reservation."

Today, the north side of the 1700 block of East Baltimore Street is a park. The row house where Aunt Jeanette stayed that first summer in 1957 is no more. Old Sid's Ranch House is a vacant lot. A 1973 advertisement in the *Baltimore Sun* announced the public auction, held on the premises, to sell all of the restaurant fixtures and equipment of the Moonlight to the highest bidder.

It read, "Forced To Vacate Due To Urban Renewal Activity Neighborhood Improvement Project."

George Vasiliades, the nephew of the owner of the Moonlight, struck out on his own as a young man in 1965. He bought the restaurant that—before the gentrification of the southeast waterfront—was a virtual reincarnation of the old Moonlight. Albeit much smaller, Sip & Bite, at the corner of Boston and Van Lill streets, has been serving up many of the same dishes ever since. And the Indians followed George there.

For many years, Sip & Bite was a favorite after-church lunch spot for the Lumbee community, which—although not as geographically concentrated as it once was—remains in the same general area. Its members still return to the old neighborhood to visit the remaining cornerstones of "the reservation." The Indian Center and two of the old churches are still going, although they too have moved a few times.

Aunt Jeanette is now Jeanette W. Jones Although she is no longer a frequent visitor to the Sip & Bite, once in a while she and Mr. George—officially retired—bump into one another at the diner. They always say hello and regard each other kindly, fellow veterans of a different time.

Baltimore Weather

DAVID MICHAEL ETTLIN

Back in the day—back when newspapers were lush with advertising and the luxury of space to fill with stories—editors obsessed almost daily about how to feed the beast.

Imagine, it's 11:00 a.m., and those editors are gathered 'round a conference table, talking up story possibilities. A politician arrested for DWI? Great—down page on the front of Metro! Random mayhem? Excellent! Got a photo of the victim yet? Night meeting of the school board? Hold space on page two! Centerpiece? Cover art?

"It's hot out today," one says. "Maybe rewrite can gin up a weather story."

For nearly a quarter-century of my forty-year career there, I was rewrite. And there was nothing I dreaded more than being greeted at my afternoon arrival with the assignment from Mount Newsuvius: "It's hot out today. See if you can do something with it."

There were variations, of course—like, "It's cold out today. See if you can do something with it," or, "They're predicting snow tomorrow. See if you can do something with it."

Not that I could cool down a hot day in August, or warm up an icy January morn. And writing about snow before it even starts falling? Let's get real. That's crazy. That's why we have a front-page blurb with a weather forecast and half a page with forecasts and statistics and maps with curvy lines showing frontal systems threatening doom for the Land of Occasionally Pleasant Living.

Editors loved to know that "yesterday was Baltimore's seventh-hottest August 4 since record-keeping began in 1880-whatever" or that ice eventually melts.

I could do something *about* the weather. Just write a story saying snow is coming, and half the time it seemed, the storm would veer off its anticipated track. All we'd see the next day was flurries. I hated seeing my byline on stories about storms that hadn't happened yet, and wouldn't. It's like Mother Nature screwing up my journalistic credibility.

Better to fill the space with a big photo of people lined up at a hardware store bearing snow shovels, or little kids with big, drippy cones of ice cream on the steps of the Maryland Science Center. "Six-year-old twins Johnny and Bengie Smith lick to keep up with their melting treats at Baltimore's

Inner Harbor yesterday as noontime temperatures edged past 90 degrees. Today's forecast calls for even hotter weather, with no end in sight before next week."

I wrote hundreds of photo captions like that. The ones I hated most had this ending: "Article, Page 2B." Which meant I also couldn't dodge writing another damn story telling our then-200,000 readers it was hot outside.

Occasionally, though, weather stories were a hoot. Real weather stories. Worries that air conditioning demand would bring down the northeastern power grid, or that islanders on the Chesapeake were being cut off from supplies and heating oil as thickening ice halted barge traffic. And somewhere at the bottom of the Bay lies a barnacle-encrusted Volkswagen that failed to make it across the frozen waterway.

A rare tornado lifted a car across the median on Loch Raven Boulevard. My late colleague Joe Challmes dashed out to the hospital to interview the car's occupants and get me the necessary quote: "Man, it was like *The Wizard of Oz*."

As the reporter most likely to write the story, I knew, when heavy snow began falling, to pack an overnight bag and get on the road before the white stuff was fender-high. I got stuck only once, driving from my Pasadena home to the *Sun*'s old headquarters on Calvert Street—veering into the median off Route 100 in a blinding whiteout. I was using old newspapers to push snow out of my path back onto the highway when the flash-booms hit.

Thundersnow. Lightning.

I managed to get the car back in gear and steered onto an exit ramp, figuring rightly that Ritchie Highway would be easier to navigate. I got to work in about two harrowing hours.

Remember Lenny Skutnik? Probably not. But he was the star of my favorite front page. On January 13, 1982, during a blinding snowstorm, Lenny dove off a bridge into the icy Potomac to save the life of a young woman—one of just five survivors—after Air Florida Flight 90 hit Washington's Fourteenth Street Bridge and sank into the river.

I was driving to work when it happened, stuck in traffic on Calvert Street for more than an hour. I went from car to car, interviewing disgusted drivers. And when I finally reached the office to say I had some good quotes, the response was, "Great. You're writing the weather story."

So why was that my favorite front page? The entire Washington staff, it seemed, had been sent out into the snow to cover the Air Florida disaster. That story, accompanied by the photo of heroic Lenny Skutnik saving Priscilla Tirado, was credited as "Washington Bureau of *The Sun*." The only byline on the front page of January 14, 1982, was mine, on the weather story.

I had partners in my weather stories—the good folks of the National Weather Service at BWI Airport, in particular Amet Figueroa. In a summer heat wave, it was never just a Bermuda high to blame. For Amet, it was "that good old Bermuda high." He retired around 2006, before the BWI weather operations were shifted to Sterling, Virginia. I was asked to speak at his farewell party, but I was on an international vacation and instead sent a two-page compilation of Amet quotes gleaned from my years of weather stories. I heard it was a highlight of the celebration.

On one occasion, asked to write about a predicted snow in 1993, I had the bright idea of asking the weather folks at Baltimore's four TV news operations for their best guesstimate on how much would fall—which, for the Queen City of the Patapsco Drainage Area, is never easy to pinpoint. And the winner (whose forecasts I still trust in any time of weather trouble) was WBAL's Tom Tasselmyer.

My story began in classic weather yarn style:

Bread, milk, toilet tissue . . . lunch meat in case the power goes out . . . salt for the front steps and driveway . . . Darn, the hardware store's run out of shovels.

You didn't have to be a mind reader yesterday to fathom the thoughts of many Marylanders as weather forecasters flat-out used the "S" word.

But then came the unrelenting ice storms of 1994 and demand for a different front-page story every day on the same damn story.

Reporters across the newsroom were sent scurrying for fresh quotes. I blessed the day veteran reporter Bob Erlandson delivered our governor's declaration of an energy emergency, as electricity demand for home heating peaked and major users cut back . . . like the Social Security Administration headquarters in suburban Woodlawn switching to backup generators to keep its enormous computers operating. It gave me a new angle for stories beyond the tally of school days lost to weather closings.

I told a *Sun* editor that after more than two decades of writing weather stories, I was running out of ledes. I needed to hang it up, turn over the reporting to younger folks, maybe . . . finally . . . become an editor instead. And Marimow delivered on that promotion a few months later.

Did I escape? Not quite. I was night metro editor February 15–18, 2003, when Baltimore was buried by more than two feet of snow. And it was a young reporter named Johnathon Briggs who was sitting at my old rewrite desk, finding his way in the art of crafting weather stories. As it finally ended, the National Weather Service declared the three days of snow a single storm, and the 28.2 inches a record.

The city was frozen in place, schools closed, side streets buried beyond recognition, the roof of the B&O Railroad Museum collapsed under the weight of snow.

"What's my lede?" Briggs asked.

"It really was the big one," I replied.

That was even good enough for the streamer headline across the front page.

A good memory, too, of times when newspapers still had money and a big staff, and Baltimore had snow in wintertime.

Houses of Ice, 1969

AFAA WEAVER

I. Ice Maker

Ice maker, ice maker, make me a block . . .
I'd holler out to Romie in the other room
where he sank water tanks to form ice
in the brine, three-hundred-pound blocks
he slipped onto the belt, slip, slap, slip,
slap, the belt sliding along the chute,
pulling the blocks to me the summer
men walked on the moon. In the freezer
it was a winter I had to bundle up to fight,
in an insulated coat my father used to wear
working in the steel mill where I thought
things must have been kinder because
this frozen hell was against all nature,
each block the same except for the chips
the ice hook made when I grabbed them
to feed the scoring machine. Things need
a process, a method for becoming real,
even ice, which is wise enough to return
to water, to unmask itself from the stamp
of human hands, to become mist, steam,
dried spots where it spreads itself as light
as air or nothing, not enough of it for miles
to become three hundred pounds again,
each pound the weight it takes to kiss,
or to fall in love, hoping love will last.

II. The Freezer

If desire has a most intense place, it is
the center of ice, where fire and water
sign a pact with machines. I want to want
a woman so deeply that everything I am

becomes what it is not, so that hardness
rising up with libido is free of ghosts,
of what I do not want, as if I can know
the origin of memorized ache, the body's
secret of encoding everything that happens
along the invisible walls of our cells
so no science except our hearts
can read writing on walls of flesh. I want
to be kept as resolute, as hard as even
the ice that cracks, each piece made
in the same will of mind, the same way
of being tenacious, fearless against
disaster. If there is power in want,
I want to know it and be free of doubt
to be a man who walks on what earth is,
a solidity of words stolen from dreams
cooked up in the minds of star systems
we know only because we believe
the stories pasted on night skies

where one day men walked on the moon
while I stepped from creaky place
to creaky place in the freezer, afraid
men would not believe me a man,
my heart blocks away in the bosom
of a woman I would marry and lose.
Heartache is a business of gain, of loss.

III. The Dock

Trucks would come at sunrise,
back up to the dock to have loads shoved
into them to take the ice to its job,
to be cracked, smashed, spread over
fresh bananas, lettuce, cabbage,
to hold the freshness of farmers
faraway longing to be bought.
The summer sun made a lie of ice,
and the ice fought back, shining

brightly into the face of a fire
that only lets us think we know what
it is or what keeps it. I am composed,
I am inebriated by the way work smells,
and somewhere in the corner is a boy
who slept all night on the empty dock,
no home to know, a child of children
like the one my lover and I are trying
to make, as if life is a *Monopoly* game
we will win if we own the real estate
that is real, its address a secret to us,
as big a secret as why I take work
to make myself a man, wrecked
inside as I am by the way memory

coils itself so scarred men will not
remember how it felt to be made
to back up and take in things stranger
than ice, things born in hurtfulness.

Afaa Weaver, author. Credit: Macon Street Books.

Herc Remembers Mobtown

AS TOLD TO RAFAEL ALVAREZ

Domenick Lombardozzi had never been in Baltimore before he was cast in 2002 to play the role of Thomas "Herc" Hauk, a city narcotics detective, on the HBO drama *The Wire*.

"My introduction was shooting the pilot of *The Wire* [September 2001], the first time I'd ever been there," said Domenick Lombardozzi, proud New Yorker born in 1976, a year before Jimmy Carter famously toured the South Bronx. "I stayed at a hotel with the other actors and thought it was a nice little town. Did some ride-alongs with cops and then saw a different side of Baltimore."

On those ride-alongs and from doing some research of his own, "I saw the story *The Wire* was going to tell. It kind of reminded me of the old South Bronx, walking with my mother when I was a kid, passing an erect building and next to it, rubble."

In early 2000s Baltimore, Lombardozzi found "no gray area, you either have it or you don't. But it was one of the better times in my life. Each season I lived somewhere different, and Baltimore became my second home."

Now in the hamlet of Valhalla, New York, Lombardozzi left Baltimore in 2009 after season five of the HBO show that made his name.

"When I came back in 2018, it had changed drastically. There were new hotels and office buildings [Harbor East]. I always knew the money wasn't going to the right places. I had a friend who was friends with a guy from Dolphin Street. He said he went to the guy's funeral and the neighborhood looked just like *The Wire*."

The differences between Baltimore and Los Angeles—at least on the surface of Tinseltown vs. Crabtown—need no explanation.

"In LA, everybody's in the business," said Lombardozzi, who appeared as Fat Tony Salerno in the 2019 Martin Scorsese film *The Irishman*.

"In Baltimore, I knew longshoremen, real people, people that grew up like me. And they didn't want anything from me but to hang out and maybe get something to eat. They accepted me. It's not like that in LA. That's why I don't live there."

Lombardozzi had a Sunday ritual that included attending Mass at St. Leo the Great on Exeter Street in Little Italy, sometimes with fellow *Wire* actor Dominick West, who played McNulty, and then going out for a meal.

He especially enjoyed the grilled asparagus at La Scala, where chef Nino Germano took care of his fellow *paisan.*

"I'd get an iced coffee at the Daily Grind in Fells Point and read the paper, maybe a script if I had to be on set the next day."

In each of the five seasons the show ran on HBO, Lombardozzi lived in a different neighborhood: Canton, downtown, across from the old Sunpapers Building on Calvert Street where the show's creator, David Simon, got his start.

"It's a very proud city, and the sports teams really bring people together," he said. "I was one of the few people on the show that lived in Baltimore."

Lombardozzi even fell hard for a Baltimore girl and dated her for seven years until they went separate ways.

"I still talk to the guys I hung out with there," he said. "I can still go there and make a phone call and have a place to stay."

Tough Letter to Baltimore (2019)

D. WATKINS

I love Baltimore.

That love forces me to tell the truth, and truth is: We need help.

For starters, the citizens of Baltimore, especially those in power, need to ask themselves, "What role am I *really* playing in making the city a better place?" before breaking their necks to address Donald Trump, or anyone really, over negative comments made about Baltimore City, because we are clearly not winning.

Regardless of how great anyone's intentions for the city are, we must spend some time looking at the current outcomes.

If you patrolled, ran the foundation, or held office for ten, twenty, thirty, or whatever amount of years, and the murder rate is still record-breaking and unemployment is still record-breaking and the idea of excelling is still a joke—then you should retire, quit, or move on because you are not good at your job, and you have failed these people.

There's no reason why me, my nephews, my older cousins, and my dad should be able to sit around and joke about how poor our schools were/are and how racist these cops who wouldn't dream of living in Baltimore City were/are—that's four generations of Black people making light of ongoing systemic oppression.

We can write President Trump off as a stupid racist all day, but we would be liars if we acted like our city also doesn't have serious problems. I say that as a native, as a property owner, as a person who is still burying friends who were victims of gun violence, as a person whose community work in Baltimore has been documented, as a lifelong resident and a citizen who is sick and tired of seeing poor Black people ignored.

I'm sick of crumbling schools that produce viral videos of freezing students up and down my social media timelines. I shouldn't have to donate books that teachers want to a school system in a major American metropolitan city.

I'm sick of my tax dollars paying the salaries of Freddie Gray's killers. I'm sick of my previously incarcerated friends, who were products of our city's failure, having to reenter society with little to no opportunities. I'm sick of almost every piece of infrastructure here, in general.

At times, it seems impossible for a Black person to make it here in Baltimore, a predominantly Black city, especially if you are crazy enough to dream of being an artist.

My success story of being a journalist and a *New York Times* bestselling author from East Baltimore is frequently dangled to the local students I visit, but the part about me having to travel to New York and DC weekly for work, because no publication or television station in Baltimore would hire me, is left out by the teachers fighting to inspire—and I'm not the only artist dealing with this.

Reginald Thomas II, from Northeast Baltimore, wanted to work as a professional photographer in his hometown more than anything, but he couldn't find work here. Strangely, no one had space for him. He eventually found a job shooting for the Boston Red Sox and is now the lead photographer for the San Antonio Spurs.

Lawrence Burney, from the east side, wanted to write for a major publication in Baltimore more than anything, but he couldn't find work here. Strangely, no one had space for him. He eventually found a job writing for *Vice* in New York and is now a senior editor at the *Fader*.

The inaugural Gordon Parks Foundation fellow, Devin Allen, is from West Baltimore. He spends his free time donating cameras to kids, exposing them to the power of creation and teaching them the skill of photography. We are lucky that Under Armour hired him because we probably would've lost him to New York, but what is the city going to do to keep him?

Kondwani Fidel is an award-winning poet from East Baltimore whose brilliant work has taken him across the world. He's been celebrated everywhere except Baltimore, where he is unable to find employment. We will probably lose him to New York.

These are just random Baltimore guys I pulled from my industry who loved Baltimore before it was cool to love Baltimore—but what about the rest of the city? How many talented people are we losing?

I swear it's like we can easily solve the problems but won't fix them.

And then this despicable, worthless Trump commentary has enough social power to spark a fake revolution where fake people almost sprain their fake fingers in a rush to type fake hashtags, with their little Inner Harbor selfies to proclaim their love for Baltimore—a city with problems that a hashtag with a Harbor pic will not fix.

Jumping on CNN and MSNBC to let the people on cable news know that you are from Baltimore will not fix the problems, but work will. Not goofy tweets acknowledging that work needs to be done—we know that—but quantifiable goals, receipts, not just talk.

Baltimore has the rawness, resilience, and innovative survival skills needed to be the greatest city in America, but it can't and it won't if we continue like this.

The Dead House

BRUCE GOLDFARB

Baltimore's boosters call it Charm City. John Quincy Adams is credited for the nickname Monumental City. The moniker perhaps most deserved is Mobtown. Throughout history, Baltimore's residents have demonstrated a proclivity for mob violence. In 1772, a merchant ship docked at Baltimore's harbor and brought an innovative device from India never before seen in the New World—an umbrella. Piqued by its novelty, a man purchased and opened the umbrella—coarse oiled linen stretched over rattan struts—and headed down the street. According to reports, horses were startled by the unfamiliar contraption. Women were alarmed and ran for their lives. Saloon patrons watched a crowd gather around the man and his umbrella. Rocks were thrown, and ultimately, the mob seized the umbrella and ripped it to shreds.

Charles F. Wiesenthal, a former physician to Frederick the Great of Prussia, received a taste of Baltimorean wrath. Wiesenthal built a small two-story brick laboratory behind his Gay Street home for the instruction of medical students. His lessons included the dissection of cadavers to learn human anatomy, which is a useful knowledge base for the treatment of human patients. In late December of 1788, when word of these outrageous happenings spread, a mob gathered at Wiesenthal's laboratory during a dissection. The rabble broke in and trashed the building, stole the cadaver, and paraded the body through the city.

In the fall of 1807, Baltimore physicians John Davidge, James Cocke, and John Shaw began offering a course of medical study. The doctors acquired the "waterlogged body of a criminal who drowned himself" for lectures in an anatomical theater Davidge built at the southeast corner of Saratoga and Liberty Streets. Outraged Baltimoreans descended on the night of November 21. A mob broke into the anatomical theater and destroyed it, taking the corpse to carry down the streets.

The incident moved members of the Maryland general assembly to charter the College of Medicine of Maryland—later renamed the University of Maryland School of Medicine—the fifth medical school in America, the first in the South, and first in the nation to include the study of anatomy with human cadavers in its curriculum.

The need for cadavers grew as the number of medical schools in Baltimore increased in the 1800s. Following the University of Maryland

School of Medicine were the College of Physicians and Surgeons, Washington Medical College, and what H. L. Mencken described as several "mephitic fly-by-night schools consisting principally of three or four quacks ambitious to posture as professors and a cadaver or two stolen from the Potters Field."

At one time, Baltimore was home to as many as seven medical schools.

Grave robbing was a flourishing industry in Baltimore. Fresh bodies were often harvested from the Eastern Potter's Field at the corner of Broadway and Orleans, the present location of the Weinberg-Kimmel Cancer Center of the Johns Hopkins Medical Center. The proximity of burial grounds and the B&O Railroad's Mount Clare station facilitated a brisk trade in cadavers to medical schools throughout the East Coast. Baltimore's reliability as a supplier of cadavers for anatomical study earned it the reputation as the Paris of America. In the trade, it was known as Resurrection City.

The two-story domed University of Maryland medical school building constructed in 1812 at the corner of Lombard and Greene, now known as Davidge Hall, incorporated several security features to mitigate risk in the event a mob returned. There are no street-level windows to break, and the heavy wooden front door can be reinforced from the inside. Behind a second-story wall next to Davidge Hall's anatomic theater was a hidden spiral staircase to allow medical students to escape out the back of the building. At the top of these stairs, the medical school's alumni association installed a modest exhibit of the city's grave robbing past.

Framed on the wall in this formerly hidden space is a reproduction of a letter written in 1830 from University of Maryland surgery professor Dr. Nathan Ryno Smith to a colleague at Bowdoin College in Maine regarding the shipment of three bodies in barrels of whiskey for a fee of $50. "I shall immediately invoke Frank, our body-snatcher (a better man never lifted a spade) and confer with him on the matter. We can get them without any difficulty at present," Smith wrote. The letter itemized financial arrangements. Whiskey cost 35 cents a gallon, and the barrels were $1 each. A cadaver unceremoniously unearthed without consent was worth $10.

Frank the body snatcher, who lived beneath the sloped seats of Davidge Hall's anatomic theater, sold to medical students the whiskey displaced by the body in the barrel. The same thing happened at the receiving end of the shipment. Medical students drank the whiskey after removing the corpse from the barrel. This is reputedly the origin of "stiff drink."

In 1847 Baltimore passed the first law in the nation requiring a medical doctor to attend sudden and unexpected deaths. However, no place existed to conduct an autopsy. A cursory inspection of a body might be done at police stations, the undertaker's, a hospital, or private homes. Often, no postmortem examination was performed at all.

Calls for the dignified treatment of Baltimore's dead became increasingly urgent. Baltimore coroner Hiram Greentree appears to be the first to suggest the city council consider building "a dead house, in which to deposit dead bodies" in 1861.

Greentree reported to officials that "the bodies of persons accidentally killed &c., are often interred in the Potter's Field, and taken therefrom to the dissecting rooms, before their friends are aware of their death, thus causing great anguish to families."

The proposal was referred to the council's health committee, where no further action was taken.

The following year, Charles H. Bradford, MD, commissioner of health and city physician, brought up the matter of a dead house in his annual report to the mayor and city council:

> The erection of a dead house in some central and suitable location within the city, has been so often urged upon your Honorable bodies, that we should not venture to touch upon the subject, did not circumstances of almost daily occurrence so clearly demonstrate the necessity of such an institution.
>
> Under existing circumstances, the bodies of unknown persons found dead, are ordinarily carried to some of the police stations; but as there is no suitable place of deposit at those places, they are generally removed to the public burial ground with as little delay as possible; and it not infrequently happens that the jury is had, the coffin obtained, and the body interred, even before the deceased is missed from his home; and when the body is subsequently sought for by his family or friends, it cannot always be found; such unpleasant circumstances must continue to occur so long as the city is without the convenience of a dead-house, or some means by which dead bodies may be kept for a time sufficiently long for their recognition.

In 1869, Baltimore enacted an ordinance allotting space in the new central police station, slated for construction on the eastern side of Fayette and Fallsway, for a "Morgue or Dead House for the reception and keeping for identification of the bodies of unknown persons dying within the city, and such other bodies as may be directed to be placed therein by the Coroner of Baltimore City."

Bodies remained at the dead house for twenty-four hours unless they were too decomposed for identification or known victims of infectious disease.

Persistent stories of grave robbing pushed the Maryland general assembly in 1882 to establish an anatomical board in Baltimore City to distribute unclaimed bodies for medical education. The board was authorized to "take such bodies within forty-eight hours of death . . . for the advancement of Medical Science." Despite the best of intentions, the anatomical board was not able to provide a sufficient supply of cadavers for medical schools, and the practice of grave robbing and other abuses persisted.

The only known case of burking in the United States occurred in Baltimore in 1886—Emily Brown was strangled to death. Her killer, John T. Ross, worked in the dissecting room at University of Maryland, where he sold her body for $15. The last documented grave robbing in Baltimore was in 1899.

Efforts to establish a proper morgue in Baltimore were stymied by a lack of consensus. Some argued that the morgue should be located near the center of the city, as morgues were in New York and Paris. Others contended that it made more sense to place the morgue near the waterfront, since so many decedents were victims of drowning.

One proposal suggested locating a morgue on the former city spring property on Calvert Street between Mulberry and Lexington, near the College of Physicians and Surgeons (subsequently subsumed by the University of Maryland School of Medicine).

Residents of this then upscale neighborhood objected to the presence of the morgue and the potential for traffic congestion on a major central thoroughfare. Today this location, known as Preston Gardens, is a slender park across the street from Mercy Medical Center.

Noting that there were five dissecting rooms in Baltimore where bodies were kept for weeks or longer without complaint, a faculty committee at the College of Physicians and Surgeons sought unsuccessfully to assuage concerns of the public:

A great deal has been said about the ineligibility of the Calvert-street spring lot for a morgue, and frightful pictures have been drawn of bloated and stinking corpses spreading consternation, disgust, and, perhaps contagion in their track, being carried through the city. One writer has even suggested that the fetid emanations from the morgue itself would render Calvert street unendurable as a place of business or residence, and even impassible to sensitive people . . .

As unknown persons will be killed by railroad and other accidents, or will commit suicide by means of poison, the pistol or the rope, as well as by drowning, they will never be confined to any particular part of the city, and no matter where the morgue is located some portion of the city must be traversed in conveying them to it . . .

Wherever a morgue may be located some opposition will inevitably be around among those living in that particular neighborhood.

In May of 1887, the Baltimore city council passed an ordinance to establish a morgue but made no appropriation for provide for its construction.

With no funding available for a morgue, Francis T. King, president of the fledgling Johns Hopkins Hospital then under development on North Broadway, offered to furnish and equip facilities to receive the unknown dead and provide "post-mortem examinations in medico-legal cases."

King offered to build the facility and have the Hopkins medical staff perform forensic autopsies, all at no cost to the city. His motivation for the gesture was "the desire of making the hospital as useful as possible to the city; second, the belief that the work which should be done in a morgue, and the methods which ought to be employed in medico-legal autopsies, are subjects for which it is very desirable that systematic and skilled instruction should be given for the benefit of justice and of the public."

Baltimore officials declined King's offer. City Health Commissioner James A. Steuart, MD, argued that a morgue should be under the supervision and control of the police and the health department, and that such an arrangement would be fundamentally unfair to the city's medical schools. "It would be wrong to give any one medical school the monopoly of the advantages to be derived from the use of the corpses of the unknown dead," he said. "It would be in effect saying that the Hopkins Medical University shall teach anatomy."

The need for a modern morgue became desperate. "In the name of the afflicted friends of the unknown dead, in the name of our efficient and zealous police force, and in the name of every reflecting citizen of Baltimore, I urge that this long felt want shall no longer be neglected and laid aside as a matter for future consideration," Steuart said in 1888. "A city of five hundred thousand people cannot afford to be without a Morgue anymore than she can be without electric lights."

Baltimore made major strides in the care for its dead on March 9, 1890, when Mayor Robert Davidson signed an ordinance to appoint two physicians to serve as medical examiners for the city.

Four months later, city leaders appropriated $4,000 to select "a suitable site on the water front, or easy access from the harbor, and cause to be erected thereon a building to be used as a morgue or dead-house."

The site selected for the morgue was at the foot of President Street, on the northwest corner of Lancaster. Located in the lumber district of the waterfront, the morgue was on the eastern side of Baltimore's Inner Harbor, adjacent to the mouth of the Jones Falls, an eighteen-mile-long, flood-prone stream used for commercial navigation as well as a conduit for the city's open sewers.

One of the least desirable pieces of real estate in the city, the Jones Falls effluvium and various waterfront aromas would provide olfactory camouflage for the morgue's operation.

The City Morgue at 700 Fleet Street, built in 1925. When the Office of the Chief Medical Examiner was established in 1939, this became the medical examiner's office. Credit: Office of the Chief Medical Examiner of Maryland.

Prior to designing the morgue, city health officials visited similar facilities in Philadelphia, New York, and Boston to glean ideas for Baltimore's facility. When completed in 1890, the two-story sand brick building was forty feet wide and eighteen feet deep. The building had an autopsy room, a storage room for surgical instruments, an office, a room for holding inquests, and a room for the storage of the clothing and personal effects of decedents. An additional appropriation of $500 was necessary to properly furnish and equip the facility.

"It may be said without exaggeration that no city in the country is now provided with a morgue better adapted for the uses of such an institution than the one just completed in Baltimore," the city's health commissioner reported upon completion of the facility in 1890.

All that was needed was somebody to run the place. The health commissioner noted the need to appoint a keeper or superintendent and recommended "a practical undertaker, familiar with the methods of preserving bodies and of so preparing them for preservation that identification will be easy and the sensibilities of the relatives and friends of the dead person be not shocked by improprieties and unseemly conditions of the body or its surroundings."

Initially, the morgue had an ice-chilled refrigerator that could hold eight bodies, which could be doubled up when necessary. This woefully inadequate capacity became a chronic problem over time. In late December of 1895, newly elected Mayor Alcaeus Hooper suggested several improvements during a tour of the morgue.

"Eighteen bodies were removed to the morgue Friday night—two more than the ordinary capacity," according to an account of the mayor's visit. "Of course, the bodies over and above the capacity of the morgue had to be placed wherever room could be found." Hooper recommended that a wooden shed next to the morgue be torn down and a room with a concrete floor be built to hold bodies temporarily.

Hooper also said that "there ought to be a telephone at the morgue and also at the residence of the superintendent of the morgue." He directed the health commissioner to install a telephone immediately.

Additional improvements were made to the morgue in 1898, but by the turn of the 1900s, the facility was recognized as outdated and unsatisfactory. "The building now used as a morgue is entirely inadequate and serves very poorly for the purposes intended," coroner J. Ramsey Nevitt reported to officials. He cited as an example a recent incident in which the stench emanating from the morgue caused a nearby police station "to vacate, temporarily at least, their quarters, even after every precaution had been taken, including the liberal use of disinfectants."

Surrounded by the sights and sounds of a bustling waterfront and often shrouded in smoke from passing boats and trains, it was unpleasant for members of the public to visit the morgue to identify a decedent. "The mode of access to the building and its immediate surroundings cause quite a shock to sensitive people, especially to women," Nevitt said.

The morgue was improved again in 1909 with the addition of an incinerator and a steam/formaldehyde sterilizer that passed through to a clean room. A wharf was constructed to receive bodies directly from watercraft. Another innovation introduced at the time was the acquisition of an ammonia refrigeration plant that kept bodies at a constant thirty-degrees Fahrenheit without the need for ice. The new refrigerator doubled the capacity to sixteen bodies, which was still insufficient to meet demand.

Despite the improvements made over the years, in 1917, the city sold the property on which the morgue was located to the Baltimore and Ohio Railroad, which planned to build a bridge near the foot of President Street. The B&O paid $32,000 for the property and $6,000 for the cost of a new morgue, which was temporarily located in a leased vacant lumber warehouse on the southwest corner of Fallsway and Fleet streets. The temporary relocation, which was originally to be for three months while a new morgue was built, lasted for more than seven years.

As it had years earlier, decisions about the new morgue were bogged down by disagreements about location. There was uniform consensus that a morgue was absolutely essential, but nobody wanted it near where they worked or lived. One plan that was briefly considered proposed building a morgue straddling the Jones Falls on the south side of Pratt Street, with a platform that could be lowered to receive a body directly from the water out of view from the public. By present-day geography, this is situated between the Inner Harbor and Little Italy.

In 1920, the city's building inspector unveiled another plan for a morgue spanning the Jones Falls, with a chapel and provisions to keep sixty bodies under refrigeration. The proposal was abandoned when businesses and merchants in the vicinity objected, claiming that their employees threatened to quit if forced to work near the morgue.

"Not only negroes, but white men and women would refuse to work near a place where bodies were kept in cold storage," according to a contemporaneous account.

Meanwhile, conditions of the dismal, run-down former lumber shop were widely decried. The morgue was described as a small room with dirty green painted wallboard and an old concrete floor with a drain in the middle. An office was off to one side, and beyond that, an autopsy room with a grimy white cabinet and an enameled washstand. The morgue had an icebox with eight shelves to hold bodies. There were no chairs on the entire first floor of the building.

One member of the public wrote to the newspaper to describe the experience of having to go to the morgue to identify the husband of a friend:

> Aside from the nasty, dirty and partly dangerous section, I must say that inside the room is one of the dirtiest holes in town. There is no waiting room for ladies, no chairs to sit on if anyone should become faint and no disinfectant whatever kept in the place . . .
>
> When we viewed the body we could not help seeing other bodies, for they were all in the same compartment and mostly all exposed. Bodies that were dragged out of the river and the remains of persons who were killed and mangled in accidents, both Black and white, male and female, all were in the one part, and those that had been there for a week or more had started to decompose and the worst stench filled the room, aside from the dirty can that held the old, wet and dirty clothing that was removed from the bodies . . .

In 1922, a group of coroners spoke out about the conditions at the morgue. "The administration will build a stadium that costs thousands of dollars and allow this disgrace, this hole, to exist," said southern district coroner George C. Blades, MD. "It is the worst blot on this city that I can think of. There are absolutely no facilities for work by physicians. A person dropping dead in the city streets because of heat or sudden illness is brought into this terrible place and put side by side with some decomposed body that had been dragged from the water. I feel positive that if the majority of people knew of the conditions they would rise up in their ire and demand immediate correction of the evils now existing."

"We have no decent facilities for an autopsy, not half of the proper medical instruments required, no photographic room, no room for records or files, no refrigeration plant, no plant for hot water, no night keeper and only eight shelves on which to place the dead that come here," said at-large coroner Otto M. Reinhardt, MD. "The place is absolutely filthy and unsanitary."

"I hate to take people into this building," morgue superintendent August H. Rittmiller told a reporter. "Slabs are falling down and wood is rotting. I have a scar on my leg which I will carry through life as a result of conditions here. The lower part of the stairs rotted away under me."

Although he diligently hosed the premises with disinfectant, "the stench cannot be overcome in these quarters," Rittmiller said.

In 1922, the city purchased a piece of property for a new building across the street from the temporary morgue, on the northwest corner of Fallsway and Fleet Street. The lot was located behind the Eastern Avenue Pumping Station, built in 1912. One of the last major American cities to install enclosed sanitary sewers, the sewage pumping station was the crown jewel of Baltimore's newly unveiled sewer system.

City officials announced plans to build a reinforced concrete one-story building with a capacity to hold sixty bodies, as well as a chapel and a waiting room. This vision was whittled back over time. The city's health commissioner approved plans for a facility that could hold fifty bodies in refrigeration and featured an inspection room for the purposes of body identification, an autopsy room, an incinerator for infectious and unclaimed property, and a laboratory for performing chemical analyses.

Leaders balked when the low bid for the project came in at $172,000, far more than the $65,000 that was appropriated for the morgue. Scaled-back plans that lacked a chapel and a refrigerator capacity for thirty-six bodies elicited a bid of $100,000. Ultimately, the chapel and other amenities were pared away, and officials approved plans for a facility with a capacity for sixty-four bodies, as well as a room for the identification of decedents, an autopsy room, a room for coroner inquests, an incinerator, and a rudimentary laboratory. The final budget for the new morgue was $65,000, with another $18,000 spent to acquire the property.

Even before construction was under way, Health Commissioner C. Hampson Jones, MD, complained that the morgue, although modern in design, was not as large as it should be. "We should build the morgue with a view to future needs," he said.

A manifestation of what reporters called the "jinx" that had plagued efforts to build a new morgue over the years occurred at the laying of the cornerstone of the building on June 19, 1924. With Mayor Howard W. Jackson, various elected officials, and civic leaders in attendance along with members of the press, it became obvious that nobody had made arrangements for the customary records and newspapers that were to be sealed beneath the cornerstone. Instead, the mayor, his secretary, the commissioner of health, the inspector of buildings, and members of the De Con & David construction company dropped their business cards into a box that was placed under the cornerstone.

When the morgue at 700 Fleet Street was completed and opened in 1925, $15,000 over budget, the facility inaugurated twenty-four-hour service. This location served as the Baltimore morgue, and later the office of the chief medical examiner for the state of Maryland, for the next forty-four years.

Black and White Baltimore: Thomas, Patrick, and Mary

LAWRENCE LANAHAN

On St. Patrick's Day 2021, I went looking for Patrick Gaierty.

I knew my great-great-grandfather was buried in southwest Baltimore's New Cathedral Cemetery, somewhere in section M-14. Scanning the gravestones for his name as I ascended a hill, I turned my ankle where the ground had caved in around some roots. Who knew tracking down ancestors could be painful?

I was limping among the dead because of an experience days earlier regarding my birth. Lost on a hospital campus after a dermatology appointment, I found myself in front of the labor and delivery building. *Wait*, I realized. *I was born in that exact building.* It disoriented me to see the place where I had come into existence. And now I was walking through a place where I'd likely rest after I ceased to exist.

"Two black voids, fore and aft," Vladimir Nabokov called them, one's existence between them but a "brief crack of light." At Patrick Gaierty's grave, I hoped to gain some *terra firma* in the aft-void: the very beginning of a four-generation American story that was waiting to shape me when I came through the portal.

Lucky for me, a *Baltimore Sun* obituary filled out that story. Patrick's brief crack of light arose in County Monaghan, Ireland, 195 years ago. At twenty-four, he came to Baltimore, bought a horse and carriage, and became a hackman. He acquired more horses, more carriages, more stables, and a house at 219 West Madison Street. Patrick memorized Burns and Shakespeare, and he recited to his grandchildren poetry that he'd learned as a child in Ireland.

Other *Sun* articles completed the story. Patrick's daughter Mary Elise married James Lynch, a good friend of Cardinal James Gibbons (1834–1921). The couple bought a house around the corner on Park Avenue, and their daughter—also Mary Elise—married Frederick Victor Furst Jr., the grandson of a German immigrant carpenter.

Frederick Jr. worked at a printing company his father and uncles started with equipment liquidated by another printer after the Great Baltimore

Fire of 1904. Mary Elise worked at Hutzler's department store. They had four children, including another Mary Elise: my mother.

Reading about my family in old newspapers was a thrill, but I didn't think the *Sun* alone could give me the real story of my ancestry. Where I'd get it I didn't know yet. But an old family grave seemed like a good start.

Not far from where I'd stumbled on the hill, I saw the names: PATRICK GAIERTY. HIS BELOVED WIFE JULIA.

From the cross and sacred heart of Jesus atop the gravestone, downtown Baltimore was visible, most of it built in the 110 years since Patrick Gaierty's death. It is there in that downtown, on a pungent wharf in nineteenth-century Baltimore, that another of my paths into the aft-void leads.

The story of my paternal great-great-grandfather, Thomas Lanahan, was harder to piece together. Like most Irish immigrant laborers, he didn't merit news coverage. The other Thomas Lanahan in town back then was a lawyer of enough renown to crowd my ancestor out of search results in the *Sun* archive.

Thomas's misadventures did earn him two *Sun* appearances, though. On March 1, 1861, a constable arrested him for "recklessly driving" on Commerce Street and injuring someone's horse. In 1870, the paper chronicled a dispute with a Centre Market "huckster" named William Scharf. "Lanahan, a drayman, ran his dray against [Scharf's] stall. . . . Scharf then violently assaulted Lanahan, and cut his head severely with a stone."

Patrick Gaierty's grave in Baltimore. Credit: Lawrence Lanahan.

I knew from old copies of the Baltimore City Directory that Thomas was a drayman and that he had lived right by Centre Market and Commerce Street in 1867 on McElderry's Wharf, which couldn't have smelled good, and in 1870 on Second Street, an alley so foul it was written up in the *Sun* five decades later simply for how intolerably fetid it was.

In 1855, Thomas and his wife, Mary, had a son, John, who became a blacksmith and a molder. He and his wife, Eva, settled their family at 2227 East Biddle Street in East Baltimore. Many of their siblings lived in that rowhouse, too, including one who hucked newspapers on the street (*Baltimore Sun*: "Old 'Newsy' Dead: Francis Senft, Crippel [sic], Known at Baltimore and Calvert Streets").

John and Eva eventually bought a "Foursquare house" in Northeast Baltimore, where John died in 1934. Their son Lawrence moved his two children—Lawrence Jr. and Patricia—in with Eva after separating from his wife. When Eva died in 1939, they moved in with a neighbor, then bounced between the homes of Lawrence's many siblings as he sought work during the Great Depression. Eventually, Johns Hopkins Hospital hired him as a secretary, and he remarried, taking an apartment near the Govans neighborhood.

Lawrence Jr. went to Loyola College and spent a few years in the US Navy. Then he took law school classes at night while working at a bank and started a family with his wife, Mary Elise, née Furst, whose parents had moved the family from Park Avenue in Mount Vernon to a rowhouse in Govans. After finishing law school, Lawrence Jr. commuted to Harford County to clerk for a circuit court judge, and he eventually joined a practice in Bel Air and moved there with his wife and two daughters.

Then, after all that, I was born.

I was surprised by how much I found of my family's Baltimore history. Tens of thousands of other Irish and German immigrants arrived in the mid-nineteenth century, many of them hackmen, draymen, and other anonymous laborers. But with just a few online tools—the *Sun* archives, Ancestry.com, and some old Baltimore City Directories—I was able to extend my story into the aft-void, understand more of what makes me who I am, and picture the Baltimore of my ancestors.

All across the city I see their footprints. A house on West Lanvale Street built in 1869 by my German immigrant great-great-grandfather, Joseph Furst. A three-story building on Orchard Street that housed Patrick Gaierty's livery stable. And Commerce Street, which Thomas Lanahan terrorized with his horse and dray.

So as I stood by Patrick Gaierty's grave, I saw not just today's Baltimore but many Baltimores, the settings for an American story of immigration, hard work, and upward mobility. Learning about this story is a constant pleasure and comfort.

It is also a privilege. And it is not the whole story.

I have told you a part of the story about glimpsing my ancestors' brief cracks of light. I left out what was happening in the shadows.

Among the thousands of Black people residing in early nineteenth-century Baltimore, both free and enslaved, were many draymen (like Thomas Lanahan) and hackmen (like Patrick Gaierty). White laborers actively worked to eliminate their competition, petitioning the city and the state legislature to ban Black people from working as draymen, hackmen, and as other laborers. The arrival of German and Irish immigrants also drove Black workers from these trades, leading one Black worker to lament, "The white employers no longer showed a preference for a Black drayman."

Patrick Gaierty arrived in Baltimore thirteen years before Maryland abolished slavery. Among Maryland's enslavers, by the Archdiocese of Baltimore's own recent admission, were some of the bishops and worshippers whose benevolence offered Irish Catholics like Patrick Gaierty and his descendants a solid foothold in Baltimore. Thomas Lanahan worked and lived in the heart of Baltimore's trafficking of enslaved people. On March 6, 1861, four days after the *Sun* reported Thomas's accident on Commerce Street, it ran this classified ad: "We are at all times purchasing SLAVES, paying the highest cash prices . . . . WILSON & HINDS 10 and 12 Commerce St."

Thomas Lanahan and Patrick Gaierty saw the demise of slavery, but they also witnessed their elected officials finding new ways to deny freedom to Black Baltimoreans. The year before Patrick Gaierty died, Baltimore City banned Black people from living in white neighborhoods. The Supreme Court struck down that ordinance in 1917, but it didn't get around to ordering school desegregation until my mother was sixteen and my father was nineteen. Downtown department stores like Hutzler's, my grandmother's employer, restricted Black employment to jobs like restroom attendant and maintenance worker through the 1950s.

Black women took work where society and the economy would abide them, often domestic work. My mother's parents both worked full-time—a necessity, apparently—yet they still employed a domestic. Mary Gibson worked for the Fursts for over two decades, taking streetcars from West

Baltimore. My mother loved Mary Gibson, and she cried when someone told her later in life how little Mary had earned each week.

To honestly appraise my ancestry is to have pain to accompany the joy of discovery. If Mary Gibson's descendants were to research their ancestors, their joy of discovery would be suffused with a pain I will never know.

They'd find nothing about Mary Gibson in the *Sun*, which did not deem Black life as newsworthy as white life (except in the police blotter), and it was much less likely Mary would appear in a Baltimore City Directory (especially as a woman, unless she was widowed or ran a business). Even finding family graves would prove difficult: many Black cemeteries were neglected or bulldozed.

In 2022, white parents are hectoring their school boards to shield their children from this history. Nationwide, state legislators are banning "divisive concepts" from schools, insisting no one should experience "discomfort, guilt, [or] anguish" because of their race.

But this history cannot *make* anyone feel anything. It simply is. I can acknowledge the advantages Thomas Lanahan enjoyed and even the way they cascaded through the generations to my own benefit, without feeling guilty. Call this "critical race theory" if you like, but it's simply my story, told honestly.

The Coliseum

EDGAR ALLAN POE

Type of the antique Rome! Rich reliquary
Of lofty contemplation left to Time
By buried centuries of pomp and power!
At length—at length—after so many days
Of weary pilgrimage and burning thirst,
(Thirst for the springs of lore that in thee lie,)
I kneel, an altered and an humble man,
Amid thy shadows, and so drink within
My very soul thy grandeur, gloom, and glory!

Vastness! and Age! and Memories of Eld!
Silence! and Desolation! and dim Night!
I feel ye now—I feel ye in your strength—
O spells more sure than e'er Judaean king
Taught in the gardens of Gethsemane!
O charms more potent than the rapt Chaldee
Ever drew down from out the quiet stars!

Here, where a hero fell, a column falls!
Here, where the mimic eagle glared in gold,
A midnight vigil holds the swarthy bat!
Here, where the dames of Rome their gilded hair
Waved to the wind, now wave the reed and thistle!
Here, where on golden throne the monarch lolled,
Glides, spectre-like, unto his marble home,
Lit by the wanlight—wan light of the horned moon,
The swift and silent lizard of the stones!

But stay! these walls—these ivy-clad arcades—
These mouldering plinths—these sad and blackened shafts—
These vague entablatures—this crumbling frieze—
These shattered cornices—this wreck—this ruin—
These stones—alas! these gray stones—are they all—
All of the famed, and the colossal left
By the corrosive Hours to Fate and me?

"Not all"—the Echoes answer me—"not all!
"Prophetic sounds and loud, arise forever
"From us, and from all Ruin, unto the wise,
"As melody from Memnon to the Sun.
"We rule the hearts of mightiest men—we rule
"With a despotic sway all giant minds.
"We are not impotent—we pallid stones.
"Not all our power is gone—not all our fame—
"Not all the magic of our high renown—
"Not all the wonder that encircles us—
"Not all the mysteries that in us lie—
"Not all the memories that hang upon
"And cling around about us as a garment,
"Clothing us in a robe of more than glory."

Poe Grave, Fayette and Greene Streets. Credit: Macon Street Books.

Huck and Tom in a Baltimore That is Gone

MICHAEL ZIEGLER

David walked into my sixth-grade class at Brehms Lane Elementary School—Mrs. Kenley's class. He was skinny, frightened, and lonely looking, with ears that stuck out like little pitcher handles. He was the new kid. He was from California.

During lunch break, some of us went home because we only lived a block or two away. I was one of those—so was Dave. I introduced myself to him and walked him home to his grandparents' house on Kenyon Avenue. He told me a little about himself—reluctantly. He didn't seem to be looking for a new friend to bother him with questions. But I persisted anyway. His parents were divorced. He and his mother moved here from California and they were going to live with his grandparents. His mother worked at Montgomery Ward.

I was introduced to Nana —his grandmother, a woman named Marie. She was a sweet lady, tall and big-boned. She spoke with a slight southern drawl. She smiled. She hugged me. She made us both grilled cheese sandwiches and French fries. I had never had a grilled cheese sandwich before that afternoon. And I had never heard of anybody getting French fries for lunch.

When we left the house to walk back to school, one question pestered me: What kind of deprived childhood was I living that I had never even heard of a grilled cheese sandwich before?

That afternoon, my life was changed. Because I liked Dave. And I really liked grilled cheese.

Dave's house was on the corner of Kenyon and Mannasota Avenue in Northeast Baltimore. There was a holly bush on the side of the house about waist-high that Dave had to shape up and keep trimmed—along with the lawn and his many other "chores." He was the only person I ever knew who had to do "chores." To me, "chores" were something that people in a Charles Dickens novel did.

Every Saturday, before Dave could do anything fun, he had to do his chores. He scrubbed, he cut the lawn, trimmed the edges and the hedges and bushes, raking it all up and throwing it away. He walked ten blocks up to High's Dairy Store on Belair Road to get a gallon of milk. Even though there was a corner store a block away, he had to trudge up to High's because of the nickel-deposit glass bottle that was returnable.

Dave hated chores. When I called him on Saturday to make our plans for the day, he'd grumble, "But *first* I have to do my *chores!*"

And Dave hated his grandfather. Or so he said. And he said it a lot.

Clarence was an old man. He didn't make small talk, and you didn't feel warm and fuzzy around him. He would always say hello—but usually in a way that made you feel like you were being accused of something.

If Clarence was home, he was usually seated at the kitchen table as you came in the back door of the house. I never went to Dave's front door for him. Never. I'd rap on the screen door and see Clarence sitting at the table facing the door—a Between the Acts "little cigar" in the corner of his mouth.

"Come in!" he'd call out like an old man who just spilled his soup in his lap. It sounded like "What—you again?!"

When I went in, he stared at me like I had forgotten to put on my pants. Then he'd call "David! David!" in a loud, cranky voice.

Dave's grandmother—Marie—was always over at the stove, and she'd turn around and smile and say, "Oh—hi Michael. I think David's still doing his chores."

Dave's mother, Shirley, was usually doing chores as well. Running a vacuum or dusting or scrubbing something. She always greeted me with a "Hi, honey"—and a smile and a wink. She was thin and pretty and she flirted—always.

Then Dave would bound up from the basement where his bedroom was. He had a bed down there and some furniture—an armoire and a chest of drawers. On the chest was a record player that also had a radio in it. It was usually tuned to WITH-AM radio Top 40.

The Lovin' Spoonful, the Beatles, the Rolling Stones, Paul Revere and the Raiders, and Motown Soul. Dave only had a few records and he played them to death—the Beatles' *White Album*, the Animals' *Greatest Hits* and the Lovin' Spoonful's *Greatest Hits*.

When Dave was cleaned-up from his chores to go out, we'd have to pass his grandfather sitting in the kitchen who'd snarl, "Did you finish all of your chores!?"

"Yes, sir," Dave would answer back politely—but impersonally—like he was addressing his drill sergeant.

"Did you scrub the bathroom?!"

"Yes, sir!" Dave would bark.

"What about the tub!?"

"I scrubbed the tub too, sir."

"Harumph," Clarence gruffed and shifted around in his seat at the table. "What about the laundry? Did you fold the laundry?!"

"No, sir. I didn't fold the . . ."

Then Shirley would cut in and say, "The laundry's not dry yet, Daddy. I'll fold it when it's dry."

Clarence would glare at us and snort then say, "Go ahead! Go ahead and go!"

Shirley would give us a wink and off we'd go. That was a typical Saturday afternoon at Dave's before we'd race off to do whatever twelve, thirteen, and fourteen-year-old boys did.

Dave's grandfather was an old curmudgeon, and he didn't know how to relate to teenage boys. I never saw him try to be a pal, offer advice, tell stories, or even smile. But I liked Clarence. His ways were stiff and old-fashioned. From them, you learned hard work and that the job needed to be done right. And when your work was finished, it was all right to play.

Clarence must have been in his seventies when his quiet life was suddenly changed by having his daughter and teenage grandson move in. Quite a bit of turmoil for an old man set in his ways. But he did what he had to do and from that alone a lot can be learned.

I think Dave was wrong about him, and I was always sorry he hated him so much. I thought Clarence was a good man. But he *was* a grouch. No doubt about that.

A typical Saturday went like this. We'd walk a mile or so up to Erdman Shopping Center. It was a recently built strip with a food store, G. C. Murphy's 5&10-Cent Store, a Read's Drug Store, and a branch of the Enoch Pratt Library. We'd spend hours in the library, picking out books to read. We'd read the dust jackets and covers of every single book, and the next week there'd be more that we had missed the week before.

Then we'd kill time in the G. C. Murphy's. Knocking on the goldfish tanks, poking the little baby turtles in their glass tanks, looking at the toys and sports gear. Sometimes in the winter, we'd sit and have a hot chocolate in Read's before wandering through the rest of our journey that took us to the Two Guys Department Store on Belair Road across from Clifton Park.

Two Guys sold everything—food, automotive supplies, clothing, stereos, and large twenty-seven-inch console color televisions in mahogany or cherry wood cabinets, long-playing records and 45s. In the rear of the store was a snack bar and an entertainment area. For ten cents, we'd play a game of two-player arcade bowling. You had to be sixteen to play the pinball machines so we peered over the shoulders of the bigger kids while they banged and bumped and tilted the machine.

We'd go to Gino's, a burger joint founded by Baltimore Colts' great Gino Marchetti. Hamburgers were fifteen cents, cheeseburgers were twenty cents, fries and a soda were fifteen cents each. For fifty cents we had a meal for lunch. I always elected for two orders of fries and no soda, and Dave always grimaced and said he didn't see how I could eat all of that without drinking anything.

And we talked. We complained about our parents and school and homework and couldn't wait for the day when we wouldn't have to "listen to anybody anymore" and could do what we wanted. We talked about music and television shows that were our favorites—*The Man from U.N.C.L.E* and *The Wild, Wild West.*

We rode bicycles everywhere. Dave had a three-speed English racer with a tan leather seat. Mine was a one-speed, as fast or slow as my legs could peddle it. We rode northeast out on Route 1 past Overlea when it was all farms. We rode southeast into Highlandtown and Canton with bars on every corner and bakeries in between.

Sometimes we only went as far as Lake Montebello, but we'd kill the afternoon there, skipping stones across the shimmering water from the shore.

That first summer, we'd finished elementary school and were set to go to Herring Run Junior High in the fall. We talked about what high school might be like. That was only a few years away "and those kids were big."

Would we fit in? Would we get big too? Get married? Leave home? Go to college? Go to war? Would we grow up? We looked at pretty girls and wondered.

We wanted to be detectives and carry a gun in our shoulder holster like Steve McQueen in *Bullitt.* We wanted to punch bad guys like Sinatra in *Lady in Cement.* And then kiss Jill St. John. We wanted to be cool like Dean Martin in *The Silencers.* We wanted to be Sean Connery as James Bond and drive fast cars and light cigarettes pulled from gold-plated cases and sip clear drinks from long-stemmed glasses.

During the summer, we'd push a rotary-blade lawn mower with a rake and a broom thrown over our shoulders and knock on the doors of strange homes where the lawn was ragged and long. We'd make two or three dollars a yard and split it. This included mowing, trimming, raking, and sweeping up.

Sometimes we'd argue over who was going to do what. I remember once we really got into it because neither of us wanted to rake that day. Dave grabbed a fistful of grass and pushed it into my face and yelled at me, "Rake it up, Ziegler!" I turned and walked away, leaving him with the lawn and whatever money he made from doing it himself.

Sometimes we fought like boys with headlocks and wrestling and rolling on the ground and, sometimes, with fists. Other times we fought with words and arguments and bad feelings, after which we might go days or weeks without calling each other.

But we always made it up. And I'd dial up Dave or he'd call me, and he always answered my "Hey" with a "Hey!—how's it going?" That was Dave's greeting: "Hey!—how's it going?"

In winter, we'd lug our snow shovels and knock on the same doors and have the same arguments—this time over who was going to scrape the ice off the steps.

Dave's grandparents had a house "at the shore." And Dave spent a lot of time there during the first few summers I knew him. I believe the house was on the Magothy River in Anne Arundel County. I thank Dave for inviting me there to spend what I now look back on as being the best week of summer in my childhood.

Clarence drove us there in his light blue Chrysler Newport. I can't remember a thing about the drive, but I remember that big house. There was a pier in back and off the pier were crab pots that Clarence and their live-in handyman, Mr. Lawrence, put out. And there was a whole lot of lawn to mow around the property. The chores at the shore were on a much larger scale.

Dave had a bedroom in the attic of the shore house. It was a large attic—with plenty of room for two boys to stand up and walk around in. There was a large door on a spring in the floor like a trapdoor that led down into the rest of the house. It was a real hideaway.

The room had a double bed that Dave and I slept in that week. There was no air-conditioning, and the room must have been hot from the August sun, but I have no memory of it. There was a fan and a few small windows. There was no TV, but we had a transistor radio that we listened to at night. In between songs we liked, we talked and we laughed and we made plans for the next day. It was 1966. Dave had just turned thirteen. I was still twelve for another few weeks. Dave was now officially a teenager and he liked to brag about it while he could.

It was the summer of 1966, and we only had the next summer day on our mind as we fell asleep in the darkness of the upstairs room while

"Paperback Writer" crackled on the radio on the nightstand. Outside in the warm, humid August night, crickets chirped in dewy grass, and sunfish splashed in the mud-colored river.

We were up and dressed and ready for the day by 7:00 a.m., and even though it was early, his grandmother was up and in the kitchen, where sausages and scrambled eggs and toast and marmalade and cold orange juice waited for us.

Sometimes we'd run out to the pier and pull up the crab pots to see how many had been caught the day before. Or we might throw some lines over and fish and always catch sunfish—sometimes two at a time—before throwing them back because, as Clarence said, they "weren't good for anything."

Most of the time we'd jump on the bicycles that were kept in the garage there and explore back country roads. I didn't know where we were, but Dave knew his way around from the many days he'd spent alone riding and exploring. We rode nowhere for hours. Sometimes stopping at a little country store for a bottle of Coke and a bag of Mrs. Ihries potato chips because they tasted just like French Fries.

In the evening after dinner, we played gin rummy with Mr. Lawrence. The old man cheated. He tried to get us to bet some pennies on the games and then he cheated. We couldn't believe it. Then he got mad when we caught him at it and wouldn't play with us anymore.

Soon, Dave's cousin Dee showed up and she brought along a girlfriend. Dee was lanky and snooty and old enough to drive and, every chance she got, she rubbed it in our face that we were just dumb little boys with our little bikes.

Dee preened and strutted and smirked and goaded us. "Are you going to ride your little bikes today? Did you have fun playing today? What are you going to be when you grow up?"

Fate rewarded us with the honor of placing Dee in the extra bedroom just below our room in the attic. The rest of the bedrooms were spread out way into other parts of the house well out of earshot.

There was a guitar in Dave's room. Neither one of us could play a single chord or read a note of music. But that didn't stop us from playing and singing many of our own original compositions in the early morning or late-night hours.

One of our classic compositions was called "Hey Red!" And it went something like this—sung loudly and off key:

There was a guy and his name was Red.
But if there was an F—he'd be a Fred.
Say Red!—are you Fred?

The last line was howled out and was followed by a ferocious banging, twanging, and strumming of that guitar. Until Dee shouted from below and knocked on the door in the ceiling (that was now locked) and finally stomped down the hall to wake Dave's mother to complain.

All of the ensuing commotion down below could be heard by us from above, and by the time Shirley got herself up, put on a robe, and came upstairs to see what we were doing, all she found was two tired, sleepy boys who swore that Dee must be dreaming.

In another twenty minutes, when all was settled down and quiet again—except for the crickets outside—we launched into the next verse:

Now this guy Red—he cut his head.
And all through the night he bled and bled.
Say Red!—are you dead?

And again, the brutal assault on the guitar and again, Dee's banging and caterwauling at the ceiling and Shirley's investigation which yielded the same result as before.

The next morning, Dave played the Mexican Hat Dance on the guitar—which was actually him beating at the strings and sitting on the edge of the bed—while we both sang *"Da-da-da-da-da-da-da-da-da. Da-da-da-da-da-da-da-da-da. Da-da-da-da-da-da-da-da-da. Da-da. Da-da Da-dah!!"* I stomped out a dance on the wooden floor that was Dee's ceiling.

Result? Two sleepy boys. A snarling, squinty-eyed Dee. A puzzled Shirley as they shut the trap door behind them.

Later that week, Dee and her girlfriend were going out to meet up with some boys. They had showered and perfumed and dressed and polished themselves up into shiny perfection. I don't recall what we had for dinner that night, and I don't recall the sassy remarks at the table.

But I do recall that Dave and I lay in ambush in the shadows of the house, at the bottom of the steps that led to the walkway that led to the driveway that led to the sports car that led to Dee's enchanted evening—until our weapons—two buckets of river water sloshed out over the both of them—thrown from the shadows. All to the sound of empty buckets clanging to the concrete and sneakers pounding in the other direction.

After more than forty years, I can still see Dee in that split-second, frozen forever in my mind. Standing there—her hair wet with seawater and makeup running down her cheeks, with an expression of shock, anger, disbelief and resignation.

Boy did we get yelled at for that by Dave's mom and grandmother. All kinds of scolding—How could we be so mean? and, You should be ashamed of yourselves. On and on. To our surprise however, Clarence never said a word.

On another day, we almost burned ourselves alive, taking with us the garage and the yacht that was stored in it. The yacht belonged to Dave's uncle, Dee's father. Somehow Dave had knocked over a gas can, spilling the liquid all over the floor of the garage—which was as clean as kitchen linoleum. We looked at one another and tried to figure out how to clean it up.

"My grandfather will kill me," he said. We tried wiping it up with paper towels but that was useless. So in a flash of brilliance, Dave decided to burn the evidence away and he tossed a lit match onto the floor.

"Whoosh and bang" and we were surrounded by flames that licked and climbed up the walls. Flames that singed the wooden door and blocked our exit. Flames that crept along the floor toward cans of paint and fuel and the yacht.

Dave beat at the flames and jumped on them. He didn't want to get caught. I, on the other hand, took the approach of trying to get out alive. Black smoke was billowing out of the building. There was no hiding this. I climbed up on the workbench and tried to open the windows. They wouldn't open. They were nailed shut. Someone's idea of securing the garage was to nail the windows shut! Probably Mr. Lawrence.

I beat at the glass and screamed "Help! Help!!"

Smoke was everywhere. Flames chased us around the walls. Dave jumped and flailed and waved his shirt and yelled at me to shut up. Suddenly it was over. The gas on the floor had burned away without total catastrophe.

But not before Clarence and Mr. Lawrence came running and shouting with Shirley behind them, as speechless as they were stammering. She just stared at us bug-eyed while Clarence and Mr. Lawrence huffed and puffed at what we did, what we almost did, and what we never should have done.

Every boy should have one summer like Tom Sawyer. That was mine.

Soon after, I introduced Dave to my oldest friend Tom, who lived across the alley from me. The three of us were inseparable through high school and worked at a Shell gas station on North Avenue and Chester Street owned by Dave's uncles, Al and Walt.

Uncle Walt reminded us of John Wayne—the way he talked and carried himself—punching us in the arm to make a point and then saying with a drawl, "and that was with my left hand . . ."

And Al was the absent-minded professor—a master at automotive transmissions despite being the type of person who would search for an hour to find his glasses that he was already wearing.

There was Turk—a narcoleptic mechanic with a thick mustache and a penchant for falling asleep while in mid-conversation. Jesse—a doughy man who was a little too fond of young teenage boys.

Richard was gangly and wore a pistol tucked in his waist. He acted like a tough guy until one day when Dave got in an argument with a customer over a parked car, and the customer pulled a revolver out of his pocket and stuck the barrel into Dave's head, shouting, "I'm going to kill you, baby! I'm going to kill you!"

Richard hightailed it into the men's room, leaving Tom and I —and a peeing-his-pants-frightened Dave—to defuse the situation.

Then there was Mister George—one of the only two white men who worked there besides us. He was fond of emptying pounds of change from the Coke machines into his pockets every day.

And one-armed John—the other white guy—who looked like Bob Hope's sidekick, Jerry Colonna. He didn't wash his uniforms too often but was a heck of a nice guy.

When we were fourteen and fifteen years old, we used to ride the bus for fifteen cents on Saturday afternoons and spend the day downtown. All the stores: Hecht's, Hutzlers, Stewarts, Brager-Gutman's, Kresge's, McCrory's, Grant's and lunch at the Earl of Sandwich, a Howard Street deli that sold real roast beef sandwiches, pouches of tater tots, apple turnovers, and birch beer.

One time, Dave and I bought a bottle of stinky perfume at a little joke store on Park Avenue and sprinkled some of the wretched liquid on the carpet in a department store elevator. The odor of rotten eggs quickly overtook the small car and at the very next floor, two very attractive young women got on.

There we were, somewhere between housewares and menswear, adolescence and childhood—two embarrassed boys who wanted to be James Bond—looking instead like a couple of bozos. The young beauties looked us over like we had just climbed out of a sludge tank with dead fish hanging out of our pants. Dave blamed me for that—and rightfully so. I was always the joker.

I remember a summer day when we took the bus downtown and a drunk named Jimmy got on somewhere along the way. Jimmy took a liking to Dave—sitting next to him and hugging and slobbering on him and kissing his cheeks, saying, "I luv yew David" all the way into the shopping district.

Then as we sat in the Earl of Sandwich later, savoring our lunch, who should stagger in but Jimmy the drunk. He was no longer as friendly as he was on the bus a few hours earlier—the cheap wine obviously wearing off. He accosted a few of the customers, demanding food until he got to us, whereupon he demanded David's pickle. Dave had spent an extra dime for a large Kosher dill and Jimmy took a shine to it.

"Let me have your pickle," he said to Dave.

Dave refused.

"You got all that food, just give me the damn pickle, that's all—just the pickle!"

Dave said no.

Jimmy grabbed at the pickle, and Dave took it and yelled back at him to leave the pickle alone.

"Gimme the damn pickle!" Jimmy bellowed, beginning to frighten people.

"Give him the pickle, for crying out loud," I said to Dave. "It's only a pickle."

Then Jimmy picked up a butter knife and started waving it in our faces and yelling for the pickle.

"Dave—give him the pickle!" I was yelling now. Dave was hanging onto it with one hand and covering his food up with the other.

"No—I want the damn pickle!"

Finally, the police appeared and escorted Jimmy out of the Earl of Sandwich—sans pickle, angry, sweaty, and confused.

Dave crunched into the pickle, red-faced and defiant as every customer in the place stared at him.

"It's my damn pickle," he said, affirming his victory to no one in particular.

I was extremely jealous of Dave's artistic talent. I couldn't believe I knew someone so talented. He sketched charcoal drawings and threw them off like it was nothing. I had a little bit of talent and could look at a picture and try to copy it—but it would take me all afternoon and the result was disappointing.

But Dave could throw off a sketch of a twisted old tree in a moonlit cemetery right out of his head in ten minutes. I remember one oil painting he did of a phone booth with bullet holes through the glass and a phone dangling behind a bloodied hand as it slid down the glass. He thought it up one evening and painted it. I wonder what became of it.

On Saturday nights, we went to the Parkside Methodist Church for dances. We hung out and tried to look cool. But we didn't fool anyone. A lot of the older guys would drink and get high before the dance. *They were cool.*

So we did what any dumb kids would do—we pretended to be high—thinking then we'd look cool too. One night, we stood and watched the band, staggering and swaying on our feet, eyes half-closed, pretending to nod off. We weren't cool, but we looked screwed-up enough that the adult chaperones herded Dave and I into an office and wanted to know what we had taken. We sobered up quickly and stammered that we were fine, but they wouldn't believe us.

Instead of being at the dance, listening to the music, we remained locked up in an office with an old guy staring at us for hours and demanding to know what we had taken and where we had gotten it. When he finally came to the conclusion that we really were just pretending, he must have thought we were so pathetic that he booted us back out into the hall.

On another occasion, Dave asked my neighbor, a girl our age who had a huge, unrequited crush on Dave, to steal a bottle of booze from her father's liquor cabinet. Anxious to please, she complied and handed us a fifth of Old Crow whiskey one Saturday for the dance that night.

That evening, Dave and I were joined by another friend named Jay. Off we went to the park—on a cold January evening—to swig whiskey out of the bottle. I took one sip and hated the taste of the stuff. So as we passed the bottle around. I only pretended to drink. As it turns out, Dave was doing the same thing.

Between the three of us, we finished the bottle, so obviously, Jay wasn't pretending to drink. By the time we walked the few blocks from the park to the dance and from the cold January night into the hot dance hall, Jay was plastered. He was falling down, and he wasn't faking. Seeing the adult chaperone catch our eye, we quickly got him out of there and walked him around outside, literally holding him up on his feet.

He threw up many times. He fell into the mud. He fell into snowbanks. We pushed snow into his face. We pooled our cents together and bought him a Coke. He threw it up. We spent hours trying to sober up poor, trusting Jay. Jay never sobered up. We dragged him slumped across our shoulders back home at 11:00 p.m.

We took him down Mannasota Avenue, across the streets and alleys, up the steps to his porch, and opened his storm door, propping him up inside between the two doors, and knocked. Before we could run away, his father opened the door, and Jay fell face first like a dead body falling out of a closet in an Abbott and Costello movie.

Behind the door, we could see that there was a living room full of guests—all gaping-mouthed and stunned. His dad looked us in the eye and asked, "What's up, men?" He waited for an answer while Jay's mother bent over the drunken heap that was Jay, shaking him and screaming.

His dad stood there, searching my face and then Dave's, waiting for an explanation. His demeanor was calm, his expression trusting. We could only do one thing. "We found him like this," we blurted out together because we had practiced this alibi over and over during the long, cold walk home.

"Yeah—it was real hot in the hall and Jay said he was going out for some air, and when we went out to find him, he was drunk."

It was a foolproof plan and we thought we pulled it off—until 9:00 p.m. Sunday night, when Jay's mother rang my doorbell with her poor hungover son in tow. Jay had spilled his guts, and she was here to gather and confront all of the guilty parties and their parents. I had to phone Dave and his mother to come up. Shirley looked more nervous than we did. I think she was more afraid that Clarence would find out than Dave was.

Then my next-door neighbor, the one sweet on Dave, was summoned along with her parents. We were all ratted out by Jay. I was angry at Dave who had caused this whole mess because I knew Shirley was a pushover who would never do anything to punish him. She was more concerned about covering this affair up than he was.

After this, I was forbidden to be friends with Dave. This lasted about two days, and Dave and I were kicking around together again. But we never saw much of Jay after that weekend.

On a more positive note, Dave was always a good student. He studied for tests—something I never did until college. And my grades showed it—mostly Cs and Ds. Always a D in math, algebra, and geometry. Dave always scored As and a few Bs here and there. He was always on the honor roll.

Maybe it was because he was afraid of what Clarence would do if he brought home poor or mediocre grades. But more likely than not, it was because Dave was a perfectionist in many ways. That was apparent in his grades as well as in his yard work. He claimed to hate mowing and trimming and raking, but when he was finished, that lawn was sharply edged, every blade of grass raked.

And it was apparent in his personal regimen. He became interested in karate while in junior high. And he bought books by the dozen to teach himself the kicks and the techniques. He exercised religiously and worked himself up from a scrawny, skinny-armed kid to a buffed-up muscular physique.

He would shout and feint kicks and karate chops out of nowhere while Tom and I were walking with him. He was good at it—but it *was annoying* to be walking along and have somebody suddenly shout "Ah-hah!" and kick their foot up higher than your head—just missing it.

Then he'd twirl and spin and slash his arms like some villain in a martial arts movie—kicking and jumping circles around us. Until Tom—who was fifty pounds beefier and six inches taller—would finally have enough and grab Dave by his neck, choking him until he gave up.

In high school, Dave became a true babe magnet. With his shaggy mane of hair, handsome face, muscular physique, charm, intelligence, and good humor, girls were easily attracted to him. Dave wound up dating Judy—the homecoming queen. She was a pretty, Spanish cheerleader with long black hair, raven eyes, an olive complexion, hot temper, and a sweet disposition. They were together all through high school. On the weekends, Tom and I were a twosome because Dave was with Judy.

On Saturdays, when we worked together at the gas station, Uncle Walt would slug Dave in the arm and kid him about "swapping spit with that little Spanish girl."

Some evenings, we'd wait at the bus stop on Belair Road for Shirley to get off the No. 15 from her job at Montgomery Ward in southwest Baltimore. While waiting for her, we'd act out fake fights—pretending to sock one another in the jaw and the gut—reeling and falling over in the process to add to the realism. Professional wrestling had nothing on us.

We went to the schoolyard with our tennis rackets and spent all afternoon whacking a tennis ball against the brick wall of the school, taking turns swatting it back and forth. Many times, we missed it and had to jump the fence to chase it across the playground.

I began losing touch with Dave when he went away to the University of Maryland to study law enforcement. After twelve years, I'd had enough of school and stayed at home and, along with Tom, formed new friendships. We drank beer, smoked pot, and hung out. Dave was getting an education to prepare for life. We had fun and drifted.

At college, Dave made friends easily and there was no shortage of girls either. When Dave came home for the weekend, we no longer had the same mutual interests, friends, experiences. I was still skinny, dark, shy, and unsure of myself while Dave was handsome, athletic, and outgoing.

We no longer shared the same mysteries about sex and becoming adults. And Dave seemed more concerned with how he was perceived by others than I was. He wanted to impress. I acted like I didn't care.

I remember one Christmas season when he was home from college, and we went out for a couple of beers. We were at a bar called the Clark Street Garage on Charles Street. Most of the clientele was college students from Johns Hopkins University.

The music from the jukebox was loud—the Who, Led Zeppelin, Alice Cooper. When it stopped, I went to the jukebox and played Nat King Cole's "The Christmas Song."

Everyone turned to look, and Dave was mortified. He pointed at me and said out loud, "He played it. I didn't play it. He played it. Way to go, Ziegler." He was embarrassed throughout the entire song and couldn't leave fast enough.

I laughed: "If they didn't want anybody to play it, why would it be in the jukebox?"

When Dave graduated, he joined the Baltimore City Police Department. He had a badge and a gun and walked the same streets on Belair Road where we used to put on fake fights. He looked big in the uniform—grown-up.

I had gotten a job at the Baltimore Gas and Electric Company and had a steady girl—Maud—who's been my steady girl since 1971. He was a grown-up, but I still felt like a teenager with no direction in life whatsoever.

I figured it was only a matter of time before he traded the uniform in for a shoulder holster and a fast car like Steve McQueen. He had done it. I just drifted along while Dave had done exactly what we both said we were going to do—become cops. But Dave wasn't happy. Walking a beat was tough, and most of the time it was boring.

It was a miserable, icy-cold and windy night when I ran into him while he was on duty. He used his walkie-talkie and called in permission to take a dinner break. We went to the Fleetway sub shop and sat in a booth. We ate grilled cheese and French fries. I reminded him that this was what we ate for lunch the day we met. But Dave was distracted. His face was red, wind-burned, and his feet were cold. He didn't like being a cop. He almost seemed embarrassed by it.

Dave married. I married. Dave divorced. I stayed married. Once Dave married, I didn't see him much at all. He was an usher in our wedding, but his wife, though she was invited, didn't attend.

Years passed, and Maud and I ran into Dave through mutual friends. Because of the connection—which included Dave's cousin Dee, she of the long-ago water-bombing—we were invited to a party. Dave was also invited. I feared I'd only been invited so she could exact her revenge. But she was gracious and friendly and had mercy.

Seeing Dave was odd—as we hardly had anything in common anymore. He drank a lot and seemed—at least to me—loud and boisterous. But Dave could never hold liquor. Two beers and that was it.

At the end of the night, he asked me, "So when are we going to be friends again?" But it was an off-the-cuff, almost rhetorical question, and before I could answer, he was off and talking to someone else. We made vague plans to keep in touch, but I knew we wouldn't.

More years passed. I kept in contact with Shirley through Christmas cards and occasional phone calls. I worked with Dave's aunt Jean at the gas and electric company. She kept me informed when I asked about Dave. One time she told me I should call him. She said he was drinking too much and "didn't have a friend in the world."

I called once and left a message but didn't expect to hear back. On a Sunday afternoon a few weeks later, he called. The conversation was forced and strange. We tried to catch up. He sounded old on the phone—worn out. There was a lot of silence between our words.

When his aunt retired from our place of work, she wrote long notes in her Christmas cards. One year, the only thing she said was, "Nobody knows where David is."

More years passed, and I heard that Shirley had died. Young, flirty, attractive Shirley. My heart ached going to the funeral home to pay my respects. It was there that I saw Dave for the last time. He was taller than I remember, still fit. His shaggy hair was close cut but still all there, unlike mine.

He said God had poured himself into the empty spaces in his life that Dave had been filling with booze. God and Dave's new wife. Dave was happy. We walked outside and Dave took a smoke, which surprised me since he was always into physical fitness

I looked at my old friend as we chatted. He looked and sounded good, but he was different. So was I. We had become what we had always wondered about—back when we skipped stones across Montebello Lake. And we had done it from a distance. And now that distance hung between us like a curtain, even though we stood just inches away.

I loved Dave as much as two boyhood friends can love each other without saying it. I miss him now like I miss my own childhood. The time we were best of friends was really only measured in a few short years, but those years span a lifetime because that's how I carry them in my memory.

My brother still lives at my old house on Kentucky Avenue, and when I go to visit him, I drive along Mannasota past Kenyon Avenue and the house where Dave and I used to spend so much time. The holly bush is still there—it's as tall as the house now. I can see Dave outside on a summer day, shirtless, in cutoffs and sneakers, pushing the rusty lawn mower with the squeaky rotary blades. His hair damp with sweat and wearing a scowl as he thinks about his grandfather.

And from a place where there is no time, he smiles and waves when I slow down and drive by and he shouts after me, "Hey! How's it going?"

I wave back and tell him that it's going fine, Dave. Everything is going fine.

Estelle Hall Young
and the Women's Suffrage Club

JEAN THOMPSON

Estelle, young and proud.
Credit: Maryland Center for History
and Culture

Druid Hill Avenue buzzed with pride on September 21, 1920. At the West Baltimore precinct houses, taking their first steps of newly acquired enfranchisement, women arrived to register to vote.

"Out in Throngs," reported the *Baltimore Sun*. By unofficial count, more than 2,500 Black women in the city fulfilled their civic duty on that first of seven days of voter registration after the ratification of the Nineteenth Amendment.

More than 63,000 Black women statewide were immediately eligible to register. But would they? Many in Baltimore and elsewhere wondered.

The *Afro-American* newspaper reported: "Women Spring Big Surprise."

Along Druid Hill and Pennsylvania Avenues—the predominantly Black Fourteenth and Seventeenth Political Wards of Baltimore—"women were out in force to register and stayed in long lines stretching out on the sidewalk until their turn came. Old and young, beautiful and homely, they were there with bells on, so as to qualify for casting their first ballot for presidential nominees in November."

Defying expectations of naysayers who expected tentativeness among the first-time registrants, the vanguard of ready-to-vote Black women in West Baltimore "went through the process of registering as though they had studied nothing else for weeks," the *Sun* reported.

This editorial musing was not far from the reality. In fact, a Black suffrage club in the segregated city had anticipated the challenges of enfranchisement and had dedicated a phalanx of women to teaching new voters how to exercise democracy. They understood that the victory was not only in gaining the vote but in using it.

Estelle Hall Young founded the Progressive Women's Suffrage Club in Baltimore in 1915. Also known as the Colored Women's Suffrage Club, it was not a Black counterpart of Baltimore's white suffrage groups.

Young's members met in their homes on Druid Hill Avenue and mobilized their community to support the ratification of the Nineteenth Amendment. However, their circumstances were different from those of the white suffrage clubs meeting in the tony neighborhood of Mount Vernon downtown.

The West Baltimore women used their connections in Black churches and civic organizations to do more than simply win the vote. They applied the force of their combined voices to protect the voting rights of their husbands, sons, and brothers, men who faced near constant legislative challenges in Maryland after the passage in 1870 of the Fifteenth Amendment.

They fought segregation and the Jim Crow laws that restricted their movements and limited economic opportunity. They advocated for reform in public education and health. They collaborated on war relief efforts. It was a time when rocks were being thrown through the windows of Black homes when families settled near white residences.

The vote, these women knew, could be a tool of empowerment, uplift, and protection.

Only in recent decades have scholars painted a clearer picture of the hurdles faced by Young and her fellow club members in the fight for voting rights. Many Southern politicians fought the Nineteenth Amendment, with those in Maryland stating explicitly their opposition to giving Black women the vote.

The Maryland legislature rejected a series of proposals for women's enfranchisement, using the rationale that the number of Black voters should not increase. Some white suffragists suggested that legislators grant all women the vote under the banner of "equal enfranchisement" with the objective of then suppressing Black women from using it.

In Baltimore, many leading white suffragists refused to welcome Black suffragists to their cause. Estelle Young did not wait to start her own movement. Raised in Atlanta, she had graduated from Spelman College, prepared to become a teacher.

While in Atlanta, she met W. E. B. Du Bois, the sociologist, intellectual, educator, and activist. In 1905, with businessman and newspaper editor William Monroe Trotter, Du Bois founded the Niagara Movement, a precursor of the NAACP.

That movement established a women's auxiliary in Baltimore, the Du Bois Circle, which remains active in 2021. Young was among its early members and leaders. Many of the Circle's members also held leadership positions with the Progressive Women's Suffrage Club, including her Druid Hill Avenue neighbors Augusta Chissell and Margaret Gregory Hawkins.

Young's husband, Dr. Howard E. Young, Baltimore's first Black pharmacist, shared her passion for community concerns and civil rights. The pharmacy and their home on Druid Hill Avenue became centers of organizing for a vital middle-class network of innovators and uplifters.

Young set about honing her skills as an orator. Notices and articles in Baltimore's *Afro-American* provide a glimpse of her industry. She spoke at church conventions, women's federations, and meetings of Black YWCA leaders. In doing so, she gained access to additional platforms.

In 1916, at a meeting of the Women's Cooperative Civic League, Young presented about women's suffrage. The League endorsed the cause, and a series of large meetings and parlor gatherings took place. Baltimore was already on its way.

The goal was to convince voters—all of whom were men—to support women's rights. Suffrage Club members understood that their get-out-the-vote campaign would extend beyond Black families and leaders. They also needed to reach pastors, employers, and merchants.

Working together, many of West Baltimore's clubwomen succeeded in 1916 in bringing the tenth convention of the National Association of Colored Women's Clubs to the city. The group's president was Margaret Murray Washington, widow of Booker T. Washington.

With the convention came a cavalcade of civil rights activists, reformers, and community advocates of national note, all convening at Bethel AME Church. Madam C. J. Walker, the hair care entrepreneur—the nation's first female, self-made millionaire—was a featured speaker.

The national association endorsed women's suffrage and urged the formation of suffrage clubs across the country.

Young appeared before an estimated 1,000 conveners and guests in a pageant, "The Vindication of Negro Womanhood," at Oriole Park, then at Greenmount and Twenty-Ninth Street. Young represented "The Southern Woman."

Ultimately, Maryland rejected the Nineteenth Amendment, but American women became voters. As the thirty-sixth state approving the constitutional amendment, Tennessee tipped the scales by ratifying the amendment on August 18, 1920. It became law on August 26, 1920.

At that moment, Young and the Baltimore suffrage club truly demonstrated their organizing prowess. Using the *Afro-American* as a trumpet, Young called on Baltimore's Black women to prepare.

"According to Mrs. Young, the honor of the women is at stake, especially since the state of Maryland has taken such an active part in trying to keep the ballot away from women because colored women would be eligible to vote," the *Afro-American* reported.

"We women," she said, "are especially bitter against the type of white politicians who said that we would not know a ballot if we saw one coming up the street. We must register in order to vote, and we must vote in order to rebuke these politicians."

At Thursday night meetings at the negro YWCA, the Women's Suffrage Club taught Black women how to register to vote. The business would include stating one's age and address. They learned how to affiliate with a political party.

(Most Black registrants would join the Republican party; at that time, Southern Democrats objected to Blacks voting, something the women could not abide. Young would later serve on the executive committee of the Independent Republican League in Baltimore.)

Plans took shape to ensure that women could travel to the polls, including Black women living in senior housing. Meanwhile, Young visited women in Montgomery County to establish suffrage club chapters there.

According to the *Afro-American*, among the first Black women to register to vote on Druid Hill Avenue in the Fourteenth Ward was Hawkins, a Women's Suffrage Club member and leader.

About 2,500 out of some 27,000 Black women eligible to vote in the city registered on the first day. By the end of the second day, an estimated 3,700 more arrived at precinct houses, and Black women had registered in about the same numbers as men in the wards where women had organized. More would do so on the five additional registration days scheduled in October.

In florid writing that is burdened by gender and racial stereotypes considered offensive to Black people then and many of all races today, *The Sun* reported on the city's women registering to vote that first day: "Baltimore's first registration day of 1920, dawn of a new epoch in American history, came and went yesterday and womanhood began a new duty to the union, cautiously, a little timidly, but brimming with purpose and buoyed with patriotism, as befits American pioneers, whether men or women."

With critiques of their clothing and assumptions about their wealth or poverty, the reporting heaped insult on women voters-to-be, saving for Black women the special insult of conjecturing about their intelligence.

Of the quiet efficiency with which informed Black women registered to vote on Druid Hill Avenue, the *Sun* wrote, "Apparently, they had done all their thinking beforehand and had brought nothing in their heads but their lessons. It was thus possible to arrive at the conclusion that while the white women were doing their own thinking, the negro women had had their thinking done for them."

Black suffragist and civic activist Sarah Collins Fernandis fired off a letter to the editor in reply. She called out the newspaper's reliance on racial stereotypes and reminded editors and readers of the labor of Baltimore's women—Black and white—in civilian service to the city and nation during World War I.

"Social and civic betterment may lay an unquestionable claim to a united women's vote," Fernandis wrote. "For many months, strong, intelligent colored women, active in suffrage circles, have carried a message with this purpose to their sisters, and there is no doubt it has had much to do with registration results."

The Women's Suffrage Club next set its sights on Election Day. Chissell, a Suffrage Club member and leader, began writing a weekly column in the *Afro-American*, answering women's questions about voting. "A Primer for Voters" explained ballot issues such as municipal loans, as well as the mechanics of voting.

"What good will it do women to vote?" asked one writer.

Replied Chissell: "It will give women power to protect themselves in their persons, property, children, occupations, opportunities and social relations. It will enable them to get done what ought to be done."

Maryland finally ratified the Nineteenth Amendment in 1941 and did not certify it until 1958.

RECIPE:
Ralph Sapia's Crabs and Spaghetti

Ingredients:
½ dozen large crabs

Sauce:
1 small/medium onion
2 tbsp garlic (fresh or minced in jar)
1 cup Italian seasoning (McCormick or Sons of Italy)
2 cans crushed tomatoes

Directions:
Steam crabs for about 10 minutes without seasoning to dispatch them.

Make the sauce: Cover the bottom of a pot with olive oil. Add onions and let simmer; once translucent, add garlic and brown (garlic cooks quickly so watch it closely). Add tomatoes and seasoning. Cook on high heat until it comes to a rolling boil—keep stirring so the sauce doesn't stick. Once boiling, turn the heat down to a simmer and cover.

Add the crabs: Leave the claws and fins on and remove the top shell. Take off face and lungs (devil) and discard. Break the crab in half (you will have two halves with claws and fins). Put crabs in sauce, making sure to add all the fat (mustard); I also include the top shell.

Cover and bring to a slow boil and let it cook for about an hour, stirring frequently. Turn to a low heat for about 2 hours. Simmer for as long as possible (best to start in the morning so you get 8 hours). Serve and eat, being careful not to wear your nicest shirt.

The Corner of Lombard and Janney

ANDRÉE ROSE CATALFAMO

Sunday afternoon, Spring 2020. These days, it's safer to stay home. The cocoon life suits me, so I decide to get into some Sunday cooking.

I root through the cupboard of pots and pans, not really knowing what I'm looking for until I find it: the Wagner Ware cast iron saucepot that was once my Italian grandmother's.

As I hold this heavy pot, I see her: Grandmom Rose, smiling lovingly at me as she stands in her kitchen in the big end-of-row house she lived in for much of her life.

I can smell the tomato sauce she'd slow-simmer in this pot to complement her homemade ravioli or spaghetti; red sauce with a mouth-watering scent that, to us, was love.

I see her now: scattering the Formica kitchen table with flour, cranking the pasta machine, turning to the stove to dip a wooden spoon in the sauce for a taste. She was always doing five things at once, but her kitchen never seemed chaotic. Each meatball and ravioli was shaped perfectly, the sauce just the right pitch of garlicky goodness.

There she is, rolling the meatballs, cupping her hands to carefully mold each one.

Look, there's little me, plopped in my white, metal high chair, playing with a half-cooked spaghetti noodle while she sings to me.

Growing up, I spent a lot of time with Grandmom; she babysat me often, especially when I was just a toddler and my mom and dad had to go to work.

Oh, we had the best time together!

As my grandmother cooked, she'd tell me the story of Little Red Riding Hood or regale me with a rousing rendition of "How Much Is That Doggie in the Window?" while I provided the "*woof, woof*" in the chorus. Or she'd sing her favorite song, "You Are My Sunshine," with out-of-tune gusto:

Grandmom Rose was my world, and I lived in it happily, a cherished, smiling meatball of a little girl. I loved when she'd hold me close and I could touch her soft brown hair, always caught in the back in a little hairnet. She smelled of talcum and flour, a scent which comforted me. To me, she was beautiful, and in her kitchen, I felt secure.

From the time she was about six years old, Rose Caputo Catalfamo lived in the 4200 block of East Lombard Street in the Highlandtown neighborhood of Baltimore. She was born to an Italian "Calabrese" immigrant coal miner, Luigi Caputo, and his Irish wife, Mary Bardy (Maria Bardi), in Clarksburg, West Virginia, on August 31, 1914.

(Why my great-grandmother chose to call herself Mary sometimes and Maria at other times is a mystery; my best guess is that when she married Luigi, she wanted to fit in with his family.)

When Rose was two, her brother Louis was born; less than a year later, their mother died from lingering complications of that childbirth. Luigi placed the children with relatives while he searched for another wife. It didn't take long; he soon met Marietta, also a Calabrese.

They quickly married and came to Baltimore, where there was work at the steel mills. Once they were settled, Luigi sent for Rose and Louie. That's how Rose found out that she had a stepmother.

Although a picture of Mary Bardy hung in her home, Grandmom didn't remember her biological mother and always called Marietta "my mother." The stepmom was neglectful and often cruel to Luigi's children, while favoring her own boy, Ernest, born not long after she married Luigi. The Southern Italian heritage was strong in Ernie; he was dark and rugged looking, even as a child, while Rose and Louie were fairer. Mary's Irish ancestry was especially noticeable in my grandmother.

"My mother didn't love me," Grandmom told me one day when we were rolling meatballs at the kitchen table. I was eight and spending a couple of weekends a month with her. Life was often chaotic at my house; my little brother had just been diagnosed as "mentally retarded" (the term in the 1960s), and my father, who wasn't too happy about having a "flawed" son, often took out his rage on all of us. Grandmom's house was my safe haven.

When I would ask why she thought that her mother didn't love her, she'd bow her head a little and shake it slowly from side to side.

"She didn't want us around, that's all." I still remember how her hazel eyes filled with tears as she spoke.

Rose paid a high price for Marietta's neglect. While still small, she fell from a stool and broke her leg and hip. A doctor set the bones, telling Luigi and Marietta that Rose would need further surgeries to fully recover.

Marietta refused to pay for any more doctors, saying that the break wasn't that bad and would heal by itself. Thus, Rose ended up with one leg almost three inches shorter than the other and walked with a painful limp for the rest of her life.

I remember the shoes she wore; heavy black leather with block heels and one sole built up so she could walk with a more even gait. I could see that it hurt her to walk in those shoes, but when she took them off, her stride was lopsided and clumsy. One time, when I knew she was hurting and I didn't know what to say, I told her that I wished she could have an operation to fix her leg so that she could feel better.

"I have better things to spend my money on, and so do you," she replied.

Luigi went to work at Bethlehem Steel's Sparrows Point mill—once the largest in the world—and the family moved from their original home in the 600 block of East Pratt Street to an end-of-row house at 4219 East Lombard Street in Highlandtown, a heavily Italian and Polish neighborhood of Southeast Baltimore.

Despite her hardships, Rose attended school through the eleventh grade and often talked about her happy years at old Eastern High School. Yet she dropped out a year before graduation; no one really knows why. Perhaps it was the times—the Great Depression. It's not hard to imagine that an educated girl was worth less to a family than one who could bring home a paycheck.

Rose took a job at Bethlehem Steel, inspecting tin for imperfections, and also made a little money as a caretaker for many of the children on her block. That's how she got to know the Catalfamos, a large and boisterous Sicilian family of eight, all crammed into a two-bedroom row house around the corner on Janney Street.

The families became close over the years, in and out of each other's lives and houses. On Christmas Day of 1938, when she was twenty-four, Rose eloped to Ellicott City with Dominic Vincent Catalfamo, one of the middle brothers.

Not much is known about how or when—or even if—they fell in love. I do know that Rose saved her money to buy her own engagement ring, a small diamond in a simple Deco setting, with money saved from her job. I still have that ring, and it is one of my most prized possessions.

Back then, Christmas weddings were fashionable, and elopements saved the families the expense of big parties. After a quick honeymoon, Dominic and Rose settled in at 4219 East Lombard, where they lived with Rose's parents. The rear bedroom, with its view of the concrete backyard and the truck depot across the street, was their love nest.

Nicknamed "Miggles," Dominic stood five-foot-nothing and was never without a cigar and a beer. He and Rose raised three children at 4219: Carmen (my father), Louis, and Lenora. As the years passed, the marriage became turbulent and the atmosphere tense. When Dominic took the third shift, painting cars at the Fisher Auto Body plant on Broening Highway, Rose and the kids breathed a sigh of relief because they were spared his bluster and bullying.

Yet, Grandmom never badmouthed Grandpop to me. "You know, Ang, your grandfather loved you so much," she told me often, showing me pictures of Grandpop and me playing in the snow in Patterson Park.

The Grandpop in those pictures seemed happy; he wore a jaunty cap and a wide, welcoming smile as he pushed me on the swings or helped me up the jungle gym.

Look at this one! Here I am, all bundled up in my puffy snowsuit, sliding down the sliding board into my Grandpop's waiting arms. That one's my favorite.

When Grandpop died suddenly of a heart attack in 1964 (I was two), Grandmom chose to stay on Lombard Street rather than sell the house to someone outside of the family. Most of my memories of her are at 4219 in that warm, safe kitchen.

I can still see the white kitchen table covered with a vinyl tablecloth with gaudy red roses.

Against one wall was the china cabinet, gray-stained wood that held the "good" dishes for special occasions, and a matching buffet, into which she'd tuck all sorts of miscellaneous stuff: our board games, bingo chips, threads and needles and other sewing notions stuffed into a double-flapped wicker basket that must have held picnic lunches once upon a time.

On top of the buffet was a small black-and-white TV, always tuned to channel two where Grandmom's favorite soap operas and game shows played all day long. I can still picture her listening for the hall phone to ring when *Dialing for Dollars* came on, waiting for Stu Kerr or Sylvia Scott to draw her name and call to tell her that she was the grand prize winner of fifty dollars.

"If one of them calls me, I'm gonna buy you something nice," she'd say, patting my head or kissing my cheek. Every week, Grandmom hoped for the big prize, but that call never came.

In the kitchen, wood-handled cooking utensils hung from hooks on the walls, and the green and white linoleum floor was scrubbed to a shine. The white enamel gas stove hissed until she lit the pilot light and the flame flickered. When I heard that noise, I knew it was time for her to get the sauce started.

When I was still a toddler, Grandmom would give me a little piece of the meatball mix and show me how to shape tiny meatballs just so; mine always turned out a little bit lopsided while hers were perfect. Through the years, I got better and better at meatball-making, imitating her movements until one day you couldn't tell mine from hers.

It was probably around that time, when I was twelve or so, that she beckoned me to come stand next to her at the stove.

"Here, Ang, I want to show you how to do this." And so I began to learn the secrets of her sauce, which always started with a potful of meatballs.

She didn't use a written recipe, and I never found out where she learned how to make it. I doubt she learned it at Marietta's stove. I imagine she figured it out herself, trying different ingredients, experimenting with cooking times and spices until she came up with a combination that pleased her.

There's some magic in this: mix ground beef with oregano, a little parsley (fresh from her windowsill), eggs, bread cubes or crumbs, and parmesan cheese, the special extra-sharp kind she'd get from Stella's Grocery store on Eastern Avenue, now gone.

Knead the mix together, but not too much, because you don't want to toughen the meat. Roll the meatballs, palm-size for regular, tiny ones to go in a lasagna.

Sauté just a couple of cloves of chopped garlic in olive oil ("A little goes a long way," she'd say), brown the meatballs, and remove. For the sauce, brown the tomato paste (three cans, and it had to be Sun of Italy), add diced tomatoes, spices, and water, stir, and bring to a gentle boil.

Don't add sugar! Unlike many Italian nonnas and moms, Grandmom didn't put sugar in her sauce. Her secret was the fresh parmesan that she grated and sprinkled liberally across the surface of the red gravy, stirring it in quickly so that none of it melted on the sides of the pot. The cheese adds a slightly salty, savory flavor that's just delicious.

Once the sauce is bubbling, plop the meatballs back in the pot, set the stove to low, wait, stir, wait, stir, have patience.

In that kitchen, throughout my childhood, Grandmom cared for me, tucked a towel into my collar for a bib, showed me how to spin spaghetti noodles into a spoon with a fork so it wouldn't slop on my face or clothes. At her table, we played Scrabble and Sorry! as she told me stories about our family.

She'd drag me over to the giant porcelain sink to scrub my face with Ivory soap when I got too gritty playing out on Janney Street with my friends, or rock in her rocker as she let out the hems of my clothes when I'd grown another inch or two.

Most importantly, the kitchen is where Grandmom taught me to read. She'd buy Golden Books by the handful and read them to me, one after another, as I sat on her lap in the rocking chair. My favorites, judging by the wear and tear on the book covers, were *The Poky Little Puppy* and *Huckleberry Hound and His Friends*.

Oh, and Yogi Bear! Grandmom liked to say that Yogi's sidekick, Boo-Boo, was my first boyfriend.

By the time I was three, I knew words by sight, and by four, I was reading fluently and scribbling little stories onto the butcher paper that Grandmom would get from Mr. Sam's grocery down the street. Mr. Sam would always send Grandmom home from his store with a couple extra sheets of that thick white paper so that I could write and draw on it. No artist ever had a better canvas!

When I was old enough to be fascinated but not enough to really understand, we'd pore over "the little papers," the tabloids that she'd get from the newsstand: the *National Enquirer*, the *New York Post*, and, God help us, the *Weekly World News*, laughing ourselves silly at the ridiculous stories of movie stars, crazy people, and aliens.

Wonderful visits like these were common all through my growing-up years. By the mid-seventies, however, I hit high school and my overnights at Grandmom's became less frequent. I'd still see her for family dinners on Sunday, but as she got older, she seldom cooked for us anymore.

Then, Sunday dinner shifted to my parents' house in Gardenville, Northeast Baltimore, or Aunt Lenora's in Joppatowne, Harford County. And while Mom or Aunt Lenora still made sauce the old way, it never had quite the magical flavor of Grandmom's. Everyone said so.

My mother always complained that there must have been some secret ingredient in Grandmom's sauce, one that she never told us about. But I watched Grandmom make that sauce a thousand times, and I never saw her slip in anything strange. It was *her* special, magical sauce.

In Grandmom's later years, when I'd come to visit her after getting off work at the bank where I wrote loans, or one of the newspapers where I sold advertising, we'd sit and talk about days gone by and flip through the albums of baby pictures and old-timers and memories.

By that time, she wasn't cooking at all but still spent her days in the kitchen, rocking in the chair she'd had forever, the polished oak showing signs of wear. Everything about her seemed white, withered, and frail as colon cancer began to ravage her body.

When Grandmom found out that she was sick, she refused chemotherapy or any treatment other than pain relief, saying that it would be a waste of time. Instead, she waited: for a visit from a friend or loved one, by the front window for a hint of a breeze, for life to end.

Fewer and fewer people came by, and she was lonely. She'd tell me that she longed for the days of family gathering around the table, for the laughter we all shared and the warmth of the kitchen filled with love.

Pointing to a spot next to the stove, she'd say, "Ang, that's where your high chair was. I still remember you sitting there. You were such a doll."

My grandmother died in June of 1992, late on a rainy night in Baltimore. She'd been at Mercy Hospital for about a week; the cancer was consuming her, and the doctors were having trouble controlling the pain. I was thirty and living with my parents again after my divorce.

When the phone rang at 2:30 a.m., we knew she had slipped away and were shocked all the same. I wasn't surprised that she left us in that quiet way; she was so proud and wouldn't have wanted anyone to see her in her last moments of suffering.

But I see her now, her kind, loving face reflected in the shine of that old Wagner Ware saucepot.

There she is, setting the pot on the ancient gas stove, mixing up her sauce; stirring, tasting, then letting it all simmer for hours, all Sunday afternoon, until the time was just right to ladle it over spaghetti for our weekly family meal.

She's smiling at me, so happy to be cooking, so happy to be spending an afternoon with her granddaughter. And on this day, a blustery Sunday in a world she would not recognize, I make her sauce from memory.

Grandmom's saucepot.

Quality

LEN SHINDEL

A painter in white coveralls
tells his apprentice,
"Don't go cheap on brushes," son.
Buy Maryland Brush,
"They are quality."

The painter probably
doesn't think about
skilled hands,
salesmen,
office workers,
managers,
quality people
down the road,
across from Engine Co. 30
Baltimore City

The painter isn't alone.
It's 1990.
Daddy Bush,
Madonna,
Kurt Schmoke,
Willie Don.
Factory folk
only get attention
when their plants shut down.

The screaming engines,
Soot-covered firemen
sometime get noticed
fighting big fires.

But, across Frederick Ave.,
away from all cameras,
quality people,
brush
away
Tradition.
Relationships change.
New dies are set.
Filaments of the past,
gradually
replaced
with
tougher stuff,
quality stuff.

Teams,
twisted tightly,
bound
together,
realizing
each other's
strengths,
ready for stronger
stampings,
new customers,
better days.

Hard-workin' folks
cuttin' and bunchin,'
fixin' and packin,'
Making history!
Worker Owners!
This is Our plant!

Nothing comes easy.
Change never does.

Sometimes,
They fight big fires
like the folks across
the street.

But they make it
Work.
Together.
Long
After
So
Many
Others
Failed.

The machines are gone.
A new owner has padlocked
the gate.

After the last shares are distributed,
the company will be
Dissolved.

Dissolved.

Dictionary synonyms are harsh.

Harsh as the competition,
the system that leaves
worker-owned plants
"dismissed,"
"abolished,"
"scrapped,"

But

documents

won't

have

the

last

word.

This history will never be dismissed.

Thirty years will never be abolished.

Relationships will never be scrapped.

Pride will persist.

Quality people will endure.

The Proclaimers

GARY M. ALMETER

When I was a little kid, I thought people were all the same. On Sunday mornings, my whole family would attend Catholic mass, and as the priest droned on about salvation, I would take comfort in knowing that Adam West and Burt Ward—Batman and Robin on TV—were also sitting in a pew, listening to their priest drone on about salvation.

I wasn't a complete idiot—I understood that they probably didn't sit together and sat with their families, just like I did. And that the Wests surely sat in a pew closer to the altar than the Wards as the West patriarch was Batman and the Ward patriarch was Robin. I also knew that Andy Gibb, Dionne Warwick, and Marilyn McCoo of television's *Solid Gold* were also at mass somewhere, along with the Solid Gold Dancers. And John Schneider and Tom Wopat; Valerie Bertinelli and Mackenzie Phillips; Todd Bridges, Gary Coleman, Dana Plato, and Conrad Bain; Mindy Cohn, Kim Fields, Lisa Whelchel, and Nancy McKeon.

But also Nancy McKeon and Phillip McKeon from *Alice* probably had to attend church together since they were brother and sister, which dictated that Linda Lavin, Polly Holliday, Vic Tayback, and Beth Howland also went to mass with them.

No matter when they worshipped, they all went home and had a big lunch of chicken and potatoes with their families. Because people are all the same!

Later, I learned that people are different. That there are different religions, colors, creeds, hair textures, dogmas, catechisms, priorities, backgrounds, ethnicities, foods. All of it. Different. This was good! It was an introduction to the notion that we can consider people with certainty, be wrong about that certainty despite our certainty, and learn from it and grow. Differences were celebrated.

Until I learned, somewhere, that differences weren't always celebrated. They were sometimes used to scorn and stereotype and subdue. Bankers, dry cleaners, basketball players, chess players, and *Dungeons & Dragons* players were different from double Dutch jumpers, farmers, doctors, residents of Appalachia, and flutists.[1] So we get accustomed to the subdivisions. Then

---

1 Edie McClurg, the school office assistant with all the pencils in her hair, did this better than I ever could in *Ferris Bueller's Day Off*. Spike Lee did it even better in that montage in *Do the Right Thing*.

there comes a time—in our evolutionary understanding of people—when we learn that differences are good but also sometimes bad.

Then there comes a time when we try to (re)learn that we are really all the same (again).

Baltimore was on the cusp of so many things in June of 2020.

We were on the cusp of summer, awaiting rules and regulations regarding beaches and barbecues; we were emerging from two months of quarantine; on the cusp of what would surely be an inimical presidential election and an interesting mayoral one. It was also becoming clear that old ways of understanding people—ourselves and others—were no longer OK.

I looked at the global uprising in response to the murder of George Floyd with surprise, elation, concern, and a bad conscience. Prior to the murder of George Floyd, I fancied myself a good Caucasian. I love Spike Lee and Barry Jenkins, know all about Emmitt Till and the Central Park Five, watch *Atlanta* and all of Dave Chappelle's specials on Netflix. I cheered when Lupita Nyong'o won her Oscar and cheered for Colin Kaepernick, and I listen to Alicia Keys and Ne-Yo and read Colson Whitehead and Brit Bennett. I even went to hear Whitehead speak at the Enoch Pratt Free Library downtown.

There didn't seem to be a large amount of gray area in this regard. I had no Confederate flags on my truck. I didn't even have a truck.[2]

Prior to George Floyd, the forty-fifth POTUS could identify his friendships with Don King and Omarosa Manigault Stallworth as evidence—*proof*—that he wasn't racist.

Prior to George Floyd, Caucasians who declared they didn't see color and advocated for color-blindness in a color-free society were lauded.

Prior to George Floyd, mistreatment of Blacks referred to a panoply of acts—nightsticks, nooses, redlining housing projects—that were identifiable.

George Floyd made it clear that things are grayer than I realized. The fury was relentless; time did nothing to abate the sadness. This was different. The outcry of the way Black people were mistreated, underpaid, and underserved was forcing previously good Caucasians to rethink oppression and their role in it. That along with my privilege came obligations.

---

2 This is traditionally the part of the essay where I tell you that I voted for Obama twice. And would've voted for him a third time had I been able. But Jordan Peele turned this into a clumsy and inapt cliché when he had Bradley Whitford say it in *Get Out*. Which I saw in the theater.

———————

I was also on the cusp of crossing a literal street in Baltimore one June morning in 2020.

It was a sunny Sunday, the tranquil ordinariness of which was tangible amid the pandemic and the Black Lives Matter protests and the general cadence of 2020. I was walking my dog, Dave. Our beagle, Beastie, had passed away from a lung tumor in April, and Dave, a fourteen-month old German Shorthaired Pointer, required significantly more exercise than Beastie did, and my family was still navigating what that exercise looked like.

It was early Sunday, and the sun was asserting itself, letting people who had ventured outside know that they would be spending the rest of the day indoors.

I was at a crosswalk, waiting to cross York Road at Regester Avenue. I pressed the button, and by this time of the pandemic, I did so with my elbow almost instinctually. As I waited for the walking man signal, a car pulled up and stopped at the red light.[3]

The driver was a young Black man, his window down. And I heard loud music coming from the car. You know what song was playing? That song by the Proclaimers, "I'm Gonna Be (500 Miles)." The man was bopping his head up and down with sufficient vigor that I was certain that he was listening to the song intentionally. I am good at gauging enthusiasm, and this young man's passion for the song was deliberate and robust.

Additionally, I was certain that this was no accident—like he wasn't just flipping through radio stations and happened upon this one—because it was 2020 and this decades-old song was never on the radio.

York Road is a main thoroughfare connecting Towson to Baltimore. The section of York Road I was attempting to cross, just north of Northern Parkway and south of Regester Avenue, is bounded by predominantly white neighborhoods and also just a few blocks north of several predominantly Black neighborhoods.

I was reminded of Brent Staples's 1986 article "Black Men in Public Space," a piece widely anthologized in composition textbooks. First published in *Ms. Magazine* in 1986, "Black Men in Public Space" is the author's first-person account of his experience as a Black man walking the streets of a big city at night.

Staples describes various encounters that show a Black man suspected

3 How many seconds is a stop light? Thirty? Sixty? Ninety? Surely it must be some multiple of thirty. For the time we spend stopped at red lights and Don't Walk signs you'd think we would know more about how they functioned. Or someone would do that thing of when they tell you how much time you spend you spend sleeping, or eating, or watching TV, and they should do one for waiting at red lights.

of being a criminal because of his skin color. After explaining how a young white woman broke into a run upon seeing him behind her, Staples reflects: "It was in the echo of that terrified woman's footfalls that I first began to know the unwieldy inheritance I'd come into—the ability to alter public space in ugly ways. . . . Her flight made me feel like an accomplice in tyranny. It also made it clear that I was indistinguishable from the 28 muggers who occasionally seeped into the area from the surrounding ghetto."

The essay is a clear statement of the ways that a Black man experiences stereotyping. He worries about how being "perceived as dangerous" may actually put him in danger. He explains, "I only needed to turn a corner into a dicey situation, or crowd some frightened, armed person in a foyer somewhere, or make an errant move after being pulled over by a policeman.

"Where fear and weapons meet— and they often do in urban America—there is always the possibility of death."

The caution born of this fear leads Staples to take on behaviors designed to put others at ease. He keeps his distance from people who appear "skittish." He closes the essay by explaining his tactic to signal that he's nonthreatening to those he encounters on his nighttime walks. He whistles familiar classical melodies. "Virtually everybody seems to sense that a mugger wouldn't be warbling bright, sunny selections from Vivaldi's Four Seasons. It is my equivalent of the cowbell that hikers wear when they know they are in bear country."

This final sentence subtly emphasizes an important point. Staples as the hiker, the whistle a cowbell—the analogy shows that Staples is the one who is afraid. He foregrounds the Black fear that results from being the object of white fear.

This section of roadway is one where Black drivers might be inclined to cowbell.

White drivers are rarely pulled over for speeding; Black drivers are pulled over with some frequency and often by a phalanx of police cars. There's a bus that links downtown Baltimore and Towson, and at night, its interior is illuminated and you can see the passengers inside, the majority of whom are working class.

———————

You know this earworm of a song, a song from decades ago, sung by the Proclaimers, a Scottish duo who look like what Lil Wayne might eat for breakfast when the diner runs out of eggs.

They are Scottish twin brothers Craig and Charles Reid who recorded the song for their 1988 album, *Sunshine on Leith*. The song was not a hit until 1993 when it was featured in the film, *Benny & Joon*, a 1993 psychological romantic comedy film released by Metro-Goldwyn-Mayer about how two eccentric individuals, Sam (Johnny Depp) and Juniper "Joon" (Mary Stuart Masterson), find each other and fall in love. Benny (Aidan Quinn) is Joon's brother. They live together following the untimely demise of their parents.

Anyway . . .

There was something, to me, so unexpected and fresh and refreshing about this scene. It was at least something *interesting,* something to *contemplate* on a walk beset by ordinariness in a month beset by quarantine and anger and sadness and disease and death.

The sight and sound jarred me; in a good way. It's not like he was listening to some *lite rap* like LL Cool J or Run-DMC or even *Caucasian rap* like the Beastie Boys or Eminem. Or *lite R&B*—Patti LaBelle, perhaps, or Anita Baker, or Luther Vandross.

He had the car seat dropped back. He wore close-cropped hair and a striped T-shirt under a gray, zip-up hoodie. His head went to and fro with the music, digging the groove of a song I had heretofore deemed grooveless.

If I was being cowbelled, the man in the car was doing it effectively. I was immediately put at ease by the innocuous, bouncy, and highly Causcasianal sounds of the Proclaimers.

I wasn't sure if stopping to talk to the man about the Proclaimers would be helpful or hurtful when it came to understanding people. I understand that the fact that I can stop and address nearly anyone is a tenet of white privilege.

A friend told me once that I love gossip but prefer the gossip amongst and betwixt Target employees to celebrity gossip.[4] Once I heard two Dunkin Donuts workers gossiping about someone who had called in sick that day. It was fascinating. So when it was time for Dave and I to cross, I stopped about five feet from the driver's window and motioned for the young man to roll his window down.

Me: Do you like this song?

Young Black man: Yeah.

Me: That's awesome, but it's sort of surprising.

YBM: I just like that old British pop.

Me: Like Pet Shop Boys and Duran Duran?

YBM: Yeah. But more alternative—like XTC and Elvis Costello.

4 I am OK with this.

Me: Good for you, man.

YBM: (looks at me blankly, or at least not with the gratified look I might have expected and for which I might have hoped, given that he had just received my invaluable stamp of approval on his music.)

Me: Are we good here?

YBM: (smiling) Yeah, we good.

We didn't solve anything; and we didn't heal anyone and our exchange was not especially eloquent.

I wish I had had my business card with me as I would have given it to him and invited him to call me so I could get his story. It's currently not much of a story. I sound like a chump, pestering a man minding his own business because I am inquisitive.[5]

I also understand that the presumption that a Black man would *yearn* to speak with me is another tenet of white privilege. But I know there *is* a story there. A story that might even rise to the level of mystery!

What's your story, kid? Where were you going that Sunday morning? When did you know you liked Brit-pop? I feel like we'd have so much to talk about. Like has he seen the video for a-ha's "Take on Me"? Is he immune to peer pressure? Maybe that is why I like these—or why we all do—instances of when people like music that they might not be expected to like based on their appearance. They are mysteries.

There must be a word for this, besides *cowbell*—likely an absurdly specific German or Norwegian word or a derivation therefrom; a word for when you see an automobile and assume you can expect what sort of music it'll be playing and then are shocked to discover that they are playing a whole different genre of music.

Or maybe there's a word for the corollary of that scenario, when you hear music and expect to see a certain automobile or person playing or whistling it and then are shocked to discover a whole different type of person.

I think this expectation is natural in an urban environment. We move through city streets with certain assumptions, derived from lived experiences and from radio and TV and movies.

---

5 It is not lost on me, a Caucasian man who wears tons of J. Crew, that I can stop and talk to whomever I want, and they will if not happily and if not readily, then certainly obligingly. I know this. I know irony. I know that when Black men approach stopped cars driven by whites, the result is not often a congenial exchange. It's like that thing of when I go to Target and the scanner doesn't scan the price of something and the cashier asks me what the thing costs and takes me at my word; and then that same cashier asks a Black person what their thing that doesn't scan cost and then the Black person tells them and they call a manager for verification. That's happened to me twice.

We take notice when those assumptions are challenged. Maybe it's true in rural and exurban areas too.

Or maybe it is a thing unique to me. Maybe I am the only one who has that thing of when I see people listening to or making a kind of music that based on their appearance, they should or shouldn't be listening to or making.[6]

I do not think this is unique to me. We all have our versions of this. We have all seen that video of when Susan Boyle walks out onto the stage of *Britain's Got Talent* and looks like she might be insane, and Simon Cowell immediately discounts her.

But then she sings "I Dreamed a Dream" and everyone's mouth is agape, and she goes on to sell four million records. Find YouTube videos of *America's Got Talent* and watch what happens to Simon Cowell's face when a young cherubic girl walks onstage and sings a rock and roll song, or when a Black man sings a country song. There's a reason Charley Pride was a pioneer.

There was also that thing in the *New York Times* right before the 2020 presidential election where they took pictures of people's refrigerators and asked readers to guess if the refrigerator belonged to a Trump supporter or a Biden supporter. Not all Biden supporters eat arugula and fancy IPAs and Trader Joe's mango chips, and not all Trump supporters put mayonnaise on everything and eat barbecue pork and drink beer.

It takes strength to swim against the current. If you're a Black man listening to, jamming to, bopping to, wholly reveling in, the Proclaimers, then you are doing so because you must really like them.

Of course, subdivisions and conformity exist for everyone. I only know what they were like for me: the myths about what I should be and should watch and should like and should listen to. I only know the social pitfalls and the silly Caucasian-ness of the whole growing-up process that I saw. I turned out OK, but sometimes, the absurd social perversions to which Caucasians adhere produce Dylann Roof, Adam Lanza, Aileen Wuornos, Ted Bundy, Kid Rock, and Sarah Palin. And Jared Kushner. Among others. And Kyle Rittenhouse. Is it like this for everyone?

But the man in that car that Sunday morning listening to the Proclaimers and bopping his head to and fro thereto had the freedom to

---

6 I included a story like this in my startling memoir *The Emperor of Ice-Cream* about this time I was walking on the sidewalk, heard someone whistling Kate Bush's "Running Up That Hill," turned around, and was surprised to see that it was a young Black man. I wondered if I was racist and came to the conclusion that in that context, I likely was something resembling racist but more akin to the sort of racism that happens as the result of being human and developing that system of expectations and attitudes. I was beating myself up but have grown to realize that so long as we are working on attitudes regarding race, so long as we are growing, so long as we are doing the best we can, then we are OK.

do so. A sufficient amount of freedom and courage, and you can do and be whatever the hell you want to be and want to do. I remember a party I went to while living in another East Coast city. I was the only one with brown shoes on.

It's a city notorious for attracting people who want to be king of the hill, A-number one, top of the heap, etc. But it also, inexplicably, fostered conformity.

Every city has its own sound, its own cacophony that evolves into a soundtrack—the way that the sound of honking horns ricochets off buildings; the certain bell-ringing of its trains; the certain swoosh of its buses' exhaust pipes and the squeak of its buses' doors; the sirens; the jackhammers and bulldozers and airplanes.

Baltimore is not a city renowned for its musical heritage in the same way Memphis or Detroit might be, though it, like any city, has reared its share of musicians.

From Billie Holiday to Tori Amos; from Adam Duritz to Sisqo; from Good Charlotte to Wye Oak; from Cab Calloway to Frank Zappa.

It's like how Aerosmith is from Boston but their sound is not Bostonian because there is no Bostonian sound of which I am aware, save for the bang and clamor of tourists asking if they can "pahk the cah in Hahvahd yahd" in perfect harmony. From a duckboat. On the Charles River.

Many streets in Baltimore have mansions on one side, albeit the backs of mansions behind a wall, and blighted homes on the other. Baltimore just inaugurated its fourth consecutive Black mayor, the past two of whom left office following indictments. It is not uncommon to see white Baltimoreans with Ray Lewis jerseys and Black Baltimoreans in Cal Ripken jerseys.

The way race plays itself out in Baltimore is complicated. Like every city but moreso somehow. It is one of those cities—along with Ferguson, Minneapolis, Kenosha—known by many for its infamous police killing of an unarmed Black man.

Baltimore had civil unrest as a result of Freddie Gray's death in 2015. Luckily for us, Caucasian crusader Kyle Rittenhouse was only twelve when that happened and none of the protesters died. Maryland fought for the Union during the Civil War but afterwards, inexplicably, the city named many parks after Confederate generals and erected many monuments honoring them.

Perhaps it isn't so inexplicable. Perhaps it was because many Marylanders wished that they could have fought for the Confederacy. Baltimore is home to Johns Hopkins University, a near-Ivy League school, and Morgan State University, a jewel in the family of HBCUs. Baltimore is home to the Preakness which, like its precursor, the Kentucky Derby, is the epicenter of seersucker, bow ties, large hats, pastel pants, and generally horsey attire one Saturday every May. Pimlico racetrack is in a blighted, mostly Black neighborhood called Park Heights where gun violence is endemic.

Baltimore, once home to a Bethlehem Steel factory that in the 1940s and 1950s employed 30,000+ workers but that closed for good in 1997 after decades of downsizing. The white immigrants, who worked there from its founding in 1897 to the historic "white flight" of the 1960s and 1970s, were able to send their kids to college and thereby had some immunity from the cataclysmic effects of such a closing. Blacks, who began working there during the Great Migration of the late 1940s and 1950s, had yet to develop such immunity.

The way Black men driving cars plays itself out is also complicated. How many of us—perfectly good Caucasians—ever see a Black man driving a Range Rover and say to ourselves, "Oh. That man must be a successful dentist!?" Or see a white teen driving a Mercedes and say, "He must sell drugs." How many parents get incensed when they cross a crosswalk with their children and hear Cardi B.'s "WAP" blaring from a car window but readily dismiss country stars Big & Rich singing "Save a Tractor, Ride a Cowboy," blaring from a Ford F-150?

We tend to look for grand gestures, words, and actions that can be immortalized in print or bronze. We can forget there are a million tiny steps that must come before any grand gestures—a million little footsteps that lead to Iwo Jima, a flier in the student union telling kids to go to Tiananmen Square, basic arithmetic questions on the test Ruby Bridges had to pass to gain admission to the all-white school.

It all starts with something that is, at first glance, positively mundane.

Race becomes less of a mystery the more we listen, the more we talk, the more we find sameness. How mysterious to wonder what it is like to walk in someone else's moccasins but to never really be able to do so. To never live in that person's skin, never know the looks, the fear, the glances, the clutched purses. Like a blind person who has contemplated but never seen the color red, we do not know the things to which we are blind. So to learn, we must ask.

And the sameness knows no limits! People of all races want to be loved, want their kids to succeed, want to be happy. They also, sometimes, like the same music.

But while the Proclaimers man and I didn't solve or heal or speak eloquent words, maybe it was a good start. Maybe it's simple: just be interested in each other. Ask questions. Answer questions. Start conversations wherever and whenever the opportunity might present itself.

And somewhere I hope this mystery man is home listening to Aztec Camera or The The or World Party or Squeeze or New Order or whatever he wants.

Footlong Franks Becomes David Franks, MD

ROSALIA SCALIA

David Franks, circa 2005. Credit: Eric Mithen.

When a friend telephoned one Saturday afternoon in the early 2000s asking if I could give fellow writer, the late David Franks, a ride to a literary reading set for that same evening, I readily agreed. Franks lived nearby, a five-minute drive from my home in Little Italy.

I only knew Franks—who often signed Valentine's Day cards "Footlong"—from hearing his poetry at a number of the literary readings that took flight in Baltimore in the mid-1990s. At those events, many in private homes and once at a Jewish cemetery, he recited poems about lost loves, loves gone wrong, jilted lovers, and aborted love affairs.

Other poems were about how his computer understood him perhaps better than any lover, clever word games about typewriter mistakes, and one yelled at us in verse with the aid of a bullhorn: "PAY ATTENTION."

In one piece, he repeatedly intoned the word, "poontang," exploring the absurdity of the word itself, used in the past as a synonym for a woman's genitalia.

(Formally defined as "a woman or women regarded solely in terms of potential sexual gratification.")

Franks's performances, his outrageous fearlessness, his wicked humor, and his embrace of multiple media forms long before they became mainstream made him quite memorable.

In my mind, however, what made him most memorable was that he'd once played a scratchy tape of his "tugboat symphony." In this piece, he'd persuaded (with charm and cases of beer), the captains on a fleet of Baker-Whiteley tugboats near his Fells Point home to blow their whistles at intervals commanded by him, the conductor.

It was ingenious, a way to honor and shape the music of the everyday world into something ordered and special. He'd also wanted to create a similar symphony using the city's church bells, and I remember thinking what an impossible task he set for himself. And wildly creative.

With this in mind, I looked forward to hearing Franks talk about his poetry and his artistic vision during the fifteen-minute ride together to Hampden on the north side of town, where the reading would take place. Neither of us were scheduled to read that night so the short commute promised to be leisurely.

I arrived at Franks's home at the corner of Bank and Regester (proper spelling of Regester Street) Streets across from St. Patrick's Catholic Church a tad early, only to discover that he'd locked himself inside. The decorative, wrought-iron security door that guarded the alley door to his home, once a barbershop, barred his ability to leave or anyone else to enter.

With the inside door open wide and the wrought-iron door securely locked, I saw him frantically searching for keys, rifling through junk drawers, and emptying various containers holding miscellaneous stuff, and although he handed me several small keys, they all failed to unlock the door.

He handed me a bobby pin through the wrought-iron slats, confident that my lock-picking skills would prove successful. We both learned that I'd be a terrible burglar, completely inept at picking locks. Time ticked by, first edging close to the perfect minute to be on time for the reading. Then edging close to the start time.

Franks became more and more upset, worried that his girlfriend Betsy would be angry at him if he didn't show up. He began calling out to passing neighbors for help, and soon a small crowd had gathered, all focused on trying to open the security door to free Franks.

Some men in the neighborly crowd tried shaking the door free. Others rushed the door to knock it off the jamb. Others tried pulling apart the wrought-iron slats. Nothing worked, and by the time all those would-be solutions were deployed, the reading had started, and Franks was mumbling about Betsy and how angry she would be.

Then Franks called 911 and begged for help from the Baltimore City fire department, saying he was a medical doctor and was called to an emergency but was trapped inside his house. The beautiful diction of his poetry performances made "Dr. Franks" sound wholly convincing, and although the dispatcher promised to send the fire department, their arrival wasn't quick enough for David.

We soon heard the sirens of fire trucks growing closer, and the group of neighbors began clapping when the fire trucks arrived. Drawn by the sirens, still more neighbors appeared to assess the situation. It occurred to me that Dr. Franks could have called a locksmith, but that would have been costly and perhaps more time-consuming.

Dr. Franks explained his urgent need to leave to the firefighters. He described the urgent medical emergency to which he'd been summoned, and the firefighters, like the true heroes they are, resolved the situation within minutes. I don't remember how. I don't remember if they simply removed the door from the jamb or broke the lock itself or cut through the wrought-iron posts, but within minutes, the job was done.

Dr. Franks thanked them hurriedly and grabbed what appeared to be an authentic, worn, brown leather medical bag as he rushed out the door. The crowd of neighbors and bystanders cheered and clapped. I wondered if he'd searched that bag for the missing keys.

By the time we left for the reading, it was half over. It would have ended by the time we reached Hampden. On the way, he wrung his hands about Betsy being mad, and I realized that, for me, attending the reading was the goal, but for Franks, it was Betsy and only Betsy.

I didn't say much on the way. I harbored unpleasant feelings toward Franks and I didn't want to be uncivil to a guest in my car. And his Dr. Franks act flabbergasted me. It may have solved his problem but could have endangered others if a blaze had broken out while firefighters were busy opening a locked gate.

Finally, he talked incessantly about Betsy and how upset she was going to be. And I would have just enough time to drop him off and get home in time to relieve the babysitter for my grandson.

As I slowed to the curb, he threw a sideways "thanks for the ride" my way and leapt out, clutching the authentic medical bag, which had belonged to his father, a physician in Washington, DC.

With the words "Poontang" and "Pay Attention" spinning in my head, Franks sprang for the venue and his Betsy without a glance in my direction, willfully ignorant of my ruined evening.

Years afterward, I coordinated a literary reading at Red Emma's, a coffee shop and bookstore then located in Baltimore's Mount Vernon neighborhood. Despite the locked door incident—and because it seemed impossible for anyone to stay angry with Franks for very long—I invited him to be one of the readers.

By then he was battling cancer. Accompanied by Betsy, he arrived late, wearing a knitted cap to hide the hair loss and carrying that same medical bag—now filled with medicines—from our previous encounter. I had not known that he'd been sick, so his appearance shocked me.

Yet he and his performance remained vintage Franks. Much to my chagrin and the annoyance of the writers who were to have followed him, Franks ignored the time constraints, turned the event into the David Franks Show, and used up all of the allotted time.

David "Footlong" Franks—who often identified himself simply as "poet," died in January of 2010.

With him went his impish humor, onstage fearlessness, boundless energy, tugboat whistles, church bells, elegant diction, and orders to "Pay Attention." And, as well, the shining shard of light that beamed through him across sixty-eight years upon the Earth.

No Return

KONDWANI FIDEL

If I knew that a poet's life was lonely
I would've kept my words hoarded in my heart.
Would've never harmed my sleeves with intimate harmonies
Would've never tatted pain in permanent ink.

I sought refuge in emptiness.
Seen sorrows end up on a silver platter
A public crucifixion—
paid for the nails, the cross, and the hammer.

I'm at a point of no return,
while poetry carries me home.
Hands never hid in a glass
house that's thrown stones.

My demons war for me
when my back is against the wall
You better have bandwidth for beef
Or regret not going vegan,
while you're resting in peace.

Since people know what details my personal life
they act as if they know me.
They look to see what the mirror inside me reflects.
Sins too difficult to eyeball.

Sometimes I feel dead inside
Sometimes I can smell the decay
when I open my mouth
In the midst

Still, I gave y'all spare keys to my grandmother's house,
Gave y'all floor seats to behind my peephole,
let y'all walk on my carpet wearing shoes,

lay in my bed with your soiled clothes.
Gave y'all food for thought while I faced famine.
& sometimes I regret letting y'all.

If I never shared my stories would I be here today?
Would I be pulling youths off the edge?
Helping them understand the importance of reading?
And that poppin' pills ain't a portal to freedom.

Even if it might seem,
Cause in reality,
you're only as free as your last lived dream.

What keeps a rose's fragrance?
The thorn that threatens
the hand that attempts to pick it?

Imagine a scent so sweet it's
worth a nose full of blood.
Would a lotus flower hold its
beauty, if it wasn't grown from the mud?

West Baltimore. Credit: Macon Street Books.

Herbie

JULIA BEAVERS

I didn't know it yet, but the emergence of my dad's friend Herbie from below decks of his new boat in a bikini top and jeans shorts would not be the most troubling part of the day.

Even at the age of eight, I should have known better than to go out on the water with my dad and his friends. But I wanted to and probably didn't have a choice anyway. Our house was like the "Island of Misfit Toys" for adults to party. You might say they were a cool cast of characters, but most were perpetually "down on their luck."

About noon, my sister Anna and I waited in Dad's 1972 dark blue Chevy cargo van. It was early June 1986 and unseasonably hot.

Or maybe it just felt more unbearable inside that big metal box. We were waiting on our dad and his friend George Melvich to make their way off the porch. My dad was usually the first one in the van, beeping and yelling out the window for everyone to "hurry the hell up."

The hold-up was George on the front porch, packing a large plastic bag with as many Budweiser cans as he could squeeze in without it breaking. My dad was grumbling, some kind of useless advice about how to do it "right" as he did with everything. Always the self-appointed supervisor.

Dad walked in and out of the house, emptying Mom's ice cube trays into George's bag, trying to get the ice to lay evenly around the beer. Surely, he'd be in trouble with my mother for using up all of "her" ice because she would need it, and more, to water down her glasses of Carlo Rossi table wine well into the evening.

George and my dad finally finished, walked down the small hill that was our front yard, and got in the van. Dad jammed the key in the ignition, and, with its usual grind then roar, the van turned over on the second or third try as it always did. Well, not always.

Don Mclean's "American Pie" was on the radio as we pulled away. It was the first time I'd heard it. Or maybe the first time I'd taken notice.

Listening to the lines, I envisioned teenagers slow dancing. In my eight-year-old mind, anything about teenagers was fascinating. I wandered through the lines of the song and painted each lyric. I was happy that I found interest in one of these "oldies" and wondered where Dad's radio station, with which I'd suffered my entire life, had been hiding this song.

Before the song finished, we'd arrived at Merritt Park, about a mile away from our duplex in "Historic Dundalk."

The park is bounded on three sides by Bullneck Creek, a branch of the Chesapeake Bay. We parked and walked to the far end, near the boat launch. Waiting for us on the pier was Herbie—Herbie Sealover, my dad's friend since childhood—and his new boat. Herbie had been promising us a boat ride, among various other promises he'd make to the kids when he was drinking at our house.

(I'm still waiting on that computer he said he'd buy us!)

Herbie's brown, curly hair wasn't short enough to be short and wasn't long enough to be considered long. Parted down the middle, it fell just at the bottom of his ears. He was smiling, wearing the "uniform" of all the guys my dad hung around: cut-off jean shorts, old tennis shoes, and white tube socks. He was shirtless and wearing a captain's hat. His skin was dark brown from being out on the boat.

Herbie hadn't been around much lately, and it was good to see him happy. There were a lot of times we'd seen him sad. I remember him coming to sit with us in the living room, away from the adults. Drunk and crying, he would tell us about another failed pursuit of love or another lost job. Although I was only in elementary school, I knew that Herbie would never figure "it" out.

At times, Herbie would do well financially, although with my dad's crew, the bar was pretty low. Herbie's presence at our house was unpredictable except for when he was drinking.

"Off the wagon" meant he wasn't working or was about to lose whatever job he had at the moment. When he wasn't around, it meant he'd given it up the bottle once more and was productive.

Herbie was single and lived with his mother, which left him plenty of time to be at the constant party that was 2559 Liberty Parkway—our family home. He would vanish for months at a time before returning with something to show for the absence. Herbie Sealover was one of the few people in my parents' orbit who acquired "nice things." Newer cars, nice clothes. And now this boat.

We all climbed aboard. Herbie's vessel was nothing like the rowboats that our parents rented on Millers Island. This would be our first "real" boat ride, and I was excited. Really, really excited. Herbie untied the ropes, settled into the captain's chair, and turned the engine. We slowly shuttled away from the dock.

I looked at George, who was sitting at the back of the boat. The legend of George was that "they" tested LSD on him in "California" in the early 1970s. I never knew what he was like before his "trip out West."

He "mumbled" a lot and had a strange stutter. I'm not sure if he always stuttered or if it was a result of his "trip." I liked when George was around.

To me, he was otherworldly and appreciated subtle things that no one else seemed to notice. If you could catch—or understand—what he was saying. It was mostly dreamy mutterings: the trees, the sky, the water. On the boat, his demeanor seemed fitting, with all of us staring at the landscape, taking in the surroundings as George always did.

Herbie navigated out of the narrow creek into more open space. He motioned me over and hoisted me onto his lap. With his hands over mine on the steering wheel. I was driving the boat! Guiding the wheel slightly to the right and the left, I felt in control and powerful!

"If You Want My Love" by Cheap Trick played from the boat's cassette tape player.

Herbie was more forward-thinking than my dad and the other guys when it came to music, if you could call Cheap Trick "forward-thinking." But they were putting out their first albums a generation after the Beatles and the Stones. No matter who was playing, however, it was barely audible through the wind.

I don't know how long I was perched there with Herbie, but I hadn't thought of Anna at all until Herbie called her over and moved me along. She was two years older than me, so he let her sit and steer alone while he stood to the side. I was on her right, Herbie to the left. At some point, Herbie slipped below deck as Anna coasted. My dad and George were still on the stern, drinking beer and gazing over the water.

After going along smoothly, the boat bouncing in the tiny waves of the wake, we started going slower. Anna wouldn't have known how to make the boat slow down. Our instructions were limited to steering. Then, there was a muted crunching sound that got louder. The boat came to a full stop, but the engine was still running.

Anna took her hands off the wheel and froze. Dad was looking around, jabbering, but I couldn't hear what he was saying. I crawled over to look below to see where our real captain was, hoping he was on his way up. I saw Herbie, still in his jean shorts, adjusting a bikini top he'd put on. Hurriedly fiddling with the straps, he headed toward the narrow stairs and came back up.

The bikini wasn't entirely shocking. We'd already seen evidence and were given brief explanations: Herbie was a "crossdresser," or, as one of our parents' female friends said, he was a "transvestite."

He wasn't "gay" or any of the other names the guys called him. The names didn't feel hateful, more in jest. A response to something baffling and maybe even threatening to a bunch of "men's men" from Dundalk. I'm sure it felt different to Herbie.

Herbie kept this part of his life mostly to himself. Sometimes if he drank enough, he might bring out pieces of his female alter ego whom he had named "Morgan."

I never saw the "full Morgan," just bits and pieces. Morgan liked expensive things, like Herbie did. I remember inheriting her fancy, lavender bottle of Gloria Vanderbilt perfume. Herbie called my eldest sister, Sacha, aside one night and gifted her an intricately detailed bra that didn't "fit Morgan."

It didn't fit Sacha either, but it was so lavish that she has it to this day. Morgan's expensive throwaways were welcomed treasures and the most expensive gifts we'd ever been given.

One night, Anna and her friend were playing with makeup, and Herbie asked if they could do his—or Morgan's—makeup. He came back to our house shortly afterward, asking that Anna "help him" with makeup again. My mom allowed it but told him not to ask again.

I remember feeling embarrassed for him when my mom scolded him in front of us and wished that she hadn't. I felt for him and how he seemed to hurt in a different way than other people I'd been around. Like he didn't belong here, in Dundalk, or at my house. But where would he go? He was loved at our house, despite the teasing about Morgan. It was gentle, it never got ugly.

Mom was a tolerant person, but I think this was a little too "offbeat," even for our offbeat household. Despite the questionable behavior that permeated the crowd that gathered in our home—most of it fueled by pot and booze—no one seemed to understand or accept Herbie's desire to dress like a woman. It seemed to touch a nerve that no one talked about.

We liked going through Herbie's bag (he always brought his bag). My cousin Matthew and I once found a "brick" of pot and two silicone breast inserts among the stuff. Unfazed by the brick of pot, we just *had* to ask him about those other things!

Very directly, he told us what they were, added that he'd paid $60 for each and to please put them back.

Maybe he didn't want the other adults to see them, or my parents to see us playing with them. Or maybe it was because they were so expensive? Never mind the brick of pot, playing with Herbie's "fake boobs" was cause for concern!

I don't think he was embarrassed. He related to children in an almost childlike way. We put them back, and I never saw them again until the boat ride.

Now on deck in his bikini top, Herbie stood for a moment not knowing what to do. Turning the engine off, he realized that Anna had driven outside of the depth markers along the channel. We were grounded on a sandbar.

Everyone—and it seemed that everything—stood still. The adults started shuffling around, trying to figure out what to do. Anna and I didn't move. Herbie started the engine and tried to put it in reverse.

Each time he revved the engine, water would bubble and spray out of the stern. The engine was loud, but we didn't move. Herbie tried and tried.

Engine on, engine off. Putting it in reverse and then trying to go forward. Eventually it moved, but just a bit. I overheard Herbie telling Dad the engine was "taking on water." I was sure that meant we were sinking.

My heart raced, and I wanted to change everything about that day: that I'd never left the house and Mom and that I had never been left in the care of my dad. My hearing seemed to be muffled. I couldn't even cry.

The boat slowly began to drift backwards, toward deeper water. He went from the steering wheel to check the engine. Back and forth. I panicked each time he abandoned the steering wheel.

I didn't say a word. No one on the boat, I was certain, could fix this. I looked over at Anna. Tears were streaming down her face and now mine too. I was worried that she would be blamed for this.

We were moving just barely faster than the flow of the creek, racing the clock. I started to recognize some of the houses along the waterfront. I knew we had to be close to where we had started. Closer to the beginning and, more importantly, closer to the end.

In the near distance, I could see the pier that we launched from. I knew how to swim and I knew Anna could swim. I was sure that I'd swum further. We could make it back if we had to, the thought of jumping into the water just a little less terrifying than going down with the boat.

Somewhere along the way, Herbie went down to the cabin and returned without the bikini top.

As we drifted alongside the pier, Herbie jumped off and secured the boat. I grabbed his hand and he pulled me onto the pier with him, an end to our grounded maiden voyage.

Anna and I both ran toward the playground at the far end of the park. I don't remember if we talked much. I assumed Dad and George helped Herbie get the boat back on his trailer. I didn't look back to see. I wanted to go home. I wanted my mom.

Sometimes I wondered about the boat. Was it fixed? Did Herbie take it out again?

Later that summer, I asked Dad if Herbie's boat had "made it back in the water."

"No," he said.

Some years later, when I was a teenager, I left my parent's drunken parties for my own. Mom had quit drinking, so the party ebbed away at our house. I lost track of Herbie and the rest of Dad's gang.

In the early 1990s, Herbie gathered all of his Beatles records in the backseat of his shiny maroon Pontiac Firebird, which he'd parked on the lawn in front of his house. He doused everything in gasoline and set the car, the records, and himself on fire.

My mom was sobbing when she told me what happened.

The father of one of my friends, also named Herb, was doing yard work nearby. He ran over and pulled Herbie from the burning car. Herbie's skin fell from his arms, and he was in a burn unit for some time.

The first time I saw Herbie after the fire, his burns were mostly healed. There were huge, pink scars on his face, neck, and hands. He told us about his "burn survivors' meetings."

When Mom asked him about the counseling, she alluded to the fact that Herbie had done this to himself and, "weren't those meetings for fire *victims*?" Herbie didn't seem put off by the question. He seemed happy, considering what he had just put himself through.

The last I'd heard about Herbie was from my cousin Matthew, who spotted him late at night at the bus stop at the end of our street. Matthew had his new girlfriend, now his wife, in the car but stopped to take Herbie home.

Julia Beavers in the park where Herbie set himself on fire. Credit: Jennifer Bishop.

Herbie was drunk and incoherent, but Matthew knew where he lived. As he helped Herbie into the house, Matthew realized that Herbie had urinated all over himself and the back seat of the car.

The next time I saw Herbie was at the funeral parlor, in his coffin.

Woman in a Hospital Gown, Baltimore

SCOT EHRHARDT

December 2018—University of Maryland Medical Center discharges a mentally ill patient, sending her to a bus stop in thirty-degree temperatures in socks and a hospital gown.

A gauze mask dangles from her neck. She leans into the December city, socked feet and vacant eyes, and opens her mouth to expel the vowels inside her.

A man reaches for his phone. The traffic soundscape absorbs her, its inattention nearly human, a threadbare life cast yellow in the streetlight.

They know not what they do . . . Credit: Jennifer Bishop.

A Garden the Size of a Picnic Blanket

HELEN YUEN

Trying to reassure me, my friend Robbyn said, "Community will save us."

It was the fall of 2020, and the COVID pandemic was coming off of its latest peak. We had walked along the Susquehanna River valley, a short drive of undulating countryside and red barns from Baltimore.

Feeling strengthened, I asked Robbyn what lay ahead. I figured she'd know. She's the type who, after all, would start a nonprofit after a messy breakup instead of wallowing in self-pity. She had said it with such clarity that I immediately felt better. Mostly. I nodded slowly, wanting to be agreeable, and because the phrase felt right in my gut.

Still, Baltimore's kaleidoscope of block parties, puppet theater, water ballet, artist-run cooperative galleries, Halloween Lantern Parades, Kinetic Sculpture Races, and such, were muted.

All of it and more were the kind of community happenings that created, well, community. How would "Small-timore" reconnect as we kept social distance? I offered idle chit-chat to fill the space as we tumbled back to the city in the dark.

Once home in the Bolton Hill neighborhood near the Maryland Institute College of Art, I looked out at my little backyard garden. The size of a picnic blanket, it's nonetheless soothing and just big enough to make me feel a connection to nature. My house sits in an alley with other row homes, all just ten feet wide.

The block stands in almost impish contrast to the grand mansions behind them, where F. Scott Fitzgerald and other historical figures once lived. Our alley homes are built of more modest brick but retain turn-of-the-century details, like a plaque on my facade with an illustration of horses at full gallop, pulling a wagon of water barrels.

The emblem indicates that the house was insured against fire damage. Lore also has it that workers of the now defunct local mill used to inhabit these buildings and that the miniature backyards held outhouses.

Today, the plot is my unruly garden, and it was time to shore it up and tidy up. Robbyn's words were still in my head when I remembered that there was a plant exchange in Baltimore. It's an online forum where one might post an overly exuberant fig tree looking for a bigger home, or a retiring cilantro in need of a more light-filled window.

Would anyone want to trade my hibiscus for some black-eyed Susans? Maryland's state flower with its yellow blooms always reminded me of a sunny smile. To my delight, a man named Martin replied. Yes, he'd love to cull and share his virulent strain with me. And he lived in my neighborhood.

The next day, I walked down Martin's alley, which was divided by a median. The strip was overflowing with saplings and colorful flowers arching over the borders. I was headed toward the address he'd given when a cheerful voice called out from the thick vegetation in the middle of the street.

Martin stood up and introduced himself. "I live over there," he said, pointing to a house catty-corner from us. It had its own front and side gardens in full bloom. Seeing my confusion, he explained that the median was once empty, so he had adopted the whole space, and it was now essentially a street-length's raised bed of mums, lilies, daffodils, and the like.

I shyly gave him my gangly vine, along with some berries from the local farmers market, to supplement the trade.

"My husband and I *love* summer fruit. Aren't you adorable!"

Martin began darting through his yard excitedly, swinging his prosthetic leg in a gentle lope as he made cuttings. He told me what this plant was, and that; their likes and dislikes; and how to grow them.

"Here," he pressed the fresh clippings warmly into my hand. "You should have more than just black-eyed Susans."

He started back to his house to get ready for an evening out, a django jazz jam in the neighborhood after dinner, and, waving goodbye, he said, "You should come!"

The gathering was in Rutter's Mill Park, one of the pocket parks that adorn our downtown neighborhood. The small public gardens are tucked on a corner or occupy a block that's closed to traffic, beautifying the end of a street.

When I arrived, there were already a handful of neighbors lounging on the benches. In their summer dress, they looked like birds ready to fly. People carrying musical instruments began to appear: a college student studying engineering, a transplant from France, a father and son who had started guitar lessons together during the pandemic.

Some greeted each other with a warm clap on the back. Others were dropping in for the first time. They all gathered under the stone gazebo and began making music.

Those on the benches rose like marionettes once the curtain parted, twirling in sync with the rhythm, individually or in pairs. The dusk light had the garden in a golden glow.

Baltimore felt like it was coming back into existence.

Days later, potted plants appeared on the sidewalk by my house where a tree had once stood. There was a note from Martin. He recalled that I had mentioned a vacant tree well on my block, and that these plants would easily grow in there to fill the empty space.

In times of global crisis, it seems like a good time to bake. In Baltimore, I had the sense that everyone was either making carbs, eating them, or both during the pandemic. Finding a muffin was like striking gold in the early days of the epidemic and involved cruising to multiple cafes and farmers markets, often to wind up empty-handed.

Motzi Bread, a bakery that opened at the onset of COVID at the corner of Guilford Avenue and Twenty-Eighth Street, soared to local fame as customers clambered in for comforting bread, and more bread.

I decided to join the craze. The methodical black and white of a recipe card provides straightforward directions in an uncertain world. The aroma of sugar, flour, and eggs caramelizing together is calming.

I settled on making a Jewish spice cake with cloves and orange peel as a seasonal autumnal choice. The week was also Rosh Hashanah, the start of a new year. While not Jewish or particularly religious, I still felt a synchronous joy and hope embodied in the symbolic onset of another cycle.

The recipe called for honey, which stands for the sweetness of life itself and, it explained, a fresh start.

I knocked on my neighbor's door with the cake still warm from the oven. Hilary and I had been exchanging home-baked goods during the pandemic as we ate through our stress and the worldwide catastrophe. She often posted photos on social media of beautifully golden challah bread she'd made for Shabbat, or of crispy latkes for her Hanukkah celebration.

"Yum!" she texted a few minutes later. I shared the link to "Zingerman's Honey Cake."

"I love Zingerman's!" she texted back with the heart emoji. She knew of the bakery located a time zone away in Ann Arbor, Michigan, while I had simply found the recipe by chance.

Hilary had done summer coursework at the University of Michigan a few years earlier, and the cake took her back to that time. I felt like a medium who'd traversed the space-time continuum to bring my friend a taste of yesteryear.

I was beginning to see that "community" is where one creates it with others. With this in mind, I biked up to my friend Elizabeth's house after learning that her father had passed away, so that I could offer my condolences in person. While this was not a COVID death, but due to an aggressive cancer, the loss was another reminder of mortality and the fragility and epic toll of the time. As we stood on her porch, keeping a safe distance, a neighbor gently approached with a box of strawberries.

"Sorry about your dad," he said, handing her the fruit. "These are from the farm."

As he turned back to his house next door, Liz said, "I want to be a compost maven, like him." Henry was his name, and the farm he mentioned was Hidden Harvest, which I was surprised to learn was just blocks from my house. Better yet, they welcomed volunteers.

We were now a year and a half into the global outbreak of the virus, and it felt like spending time at a vibrant urban farm would continue rebuilding my sense of a city that's still alive, and a feeling of connectedness to others. I pedaled over to the garden, which sits behind a high stone wall a block from North Avenue.

The major city boulevard served as Baltimore's northern boundary through the early twentieth century. It stretches the width of the city from east to west, and the area dead center, where it bisects a main artery called Charles Street, has been a city designated arts district since 2002.

On the stretch near my house, I almost missed the urban farm. I walked around the wall and down another alley before coming upon a bright space of wildflowers and live chickens. Folks in overalls were stooped over crops as they harvested and weeded.

I joined in, eager to touch another living thing, even if it was just kale. It felt good to be working with my fellow Baltimoreans towards a tangible end. We chatted and swapped stories while completing the day's tasks. I wanted to see these people again.

Druid Hill Park, 745 acres just north of downtown, is the third oldest urban park in the country after Central Park in New York and Philadelphia's

Fairmount Park. The expansive green space has been a personal haven since I moved to Baltimore, and it became even more so during the pandemic. My customary bike loop around it passes a glass and steel conservatory built in 1888 and that's shaped like an elegant cake cover. Inside are palm trees and orchids from faraway lands.

The bike path also goes by the old swimming pools, one designated for African Americans, which is half the size of the adjacent, formerly whites-only pool. Now, pool number two has been converted into public art by renowned Baltimore artist Joyce Scott as a reminder of racism and its harm, both past and present.

On my many visits to and around Druid Hill, there were always groups of people throwing around what look to me like a Frisbee. I soon learned they were playing disc golf. With my introverted self having successfully ventured to Hidden Harvest Farm, I took a deep breath one day and approached the picnic tables where several disc golf players had gathered.

Music played and there were coolers with cold beer.

"Hi," I waved hopefully.

A man with Albert Einstein hair, slightly bowed posture, a fisherman's hat, and sandals ambled forward. His name was Norm.

"So you want to learn how to play?"

I nodded yes.

People were gathering at the picnic tables every Thursday for pick-up games. The teams formed from whoever showed up. Norm was more than a regular. He had been playing for decades and had the respect of the younger participants, who spoke reverently about his skill. He fished some discs out of the lost-and-found box for us to use. Discs were always getting flung and lost in the park, and a Thursday volunteer stood by for those who wanted to search for misplaced equipment.

Norm took me to the putting green and patiently showed me how to aim, how to compensate for a disc's natural tendency to veer in one direction, and the basic rules of the game. He coached me on throwing the disc when a tree was in the flight path. And he gently nudged me to continue practicing on my own.

I bit my lip and looked back at the party at the picnic tables happening without me—a rocking good time of tight friends laughing and smoking—as I stood alone on the green. Suddenly, a voice called out I didn't recognize.

"Helen?"

I spun eagerly to see who it was.

"Michelle, from Hidden Harvest Farm." One of the farm volunteers turned out to be a disc golf aficionado. Like me, she also had grown up in a small rural town near Appalachia. We shared similar political views, and her self-effacing sense of humor made me laugh.

The happy encounter, along with the sum of the others I had made in the months during the COVID outbreak, jolted me to remember that this was Small-timore. Its heart was still there—creative, dynamic, and with interlocking connections. I had drifted and grown estranged from my beloved city as we locked down in our homes. But community was still very much there as long as we, its residents, continued to form it. I made a new acquaintance that evening in the park. And her name is Baltimore.

The Best Bar in the World

SETH SAWYERS

Before it was the best bar in the world, I hear it was as rough-and-tumble as it gets. It was called Dizzy Issie's and was one of two hundred interchangeable corner bars in this town. Dollar drafts paid for from piles of singles stacked neat on the bar and no food unless potato chips count, a pool table upstairs, plenty of fights, smoking a click shy of mandatory. Eventually, they got rid of the pool table, added a kitchen, and now they put out a good bacon-and-blue-cheese burger, solid wings, and two kinds of jalapeño poppers.

Now it's called the Dizz, and I hope it never changes, stays open until the sun swallows Remington, Baltimore, the Earth. The Dizz is, and I've been around at least a little, the kind of neighborhood bar that almost anyone would want, cozy in an end-unit row house that, no matter where you live in town, feels like it's just up the street.

It does happen to be just up the street from where I live. The Dizz is, like its city, somewhere in the middle. The Dizz is an old baseball glove. The Dizz is an old Ford pickup that runs great.

The Dizz is to Applebee's as a New York slice is to Sbarro's. It's the real deal, its own thing, an originator rather than a facsimile. Of course, you've got your own best bar in the world, and I'm sure it's wonderful, so long as you're wonderful, and I'm hoping that you are. But, for right now, the Dizz holds the title because I say so. Maybe I can convince you.

The best bar in the world does not have a specialty cocktail menu and thank god for that, though it does have a machine that turns ice into frozen drinks. The dinner specials at the best bar in the world are handwritten and photocopied. The high-end dinner is a crab cake, and I suppose they have fish and steaks. I am reasonably sure that if you are a vegetarian, they will serve you something hot to eat.

What the best bar in the world does have is a Kelly, a Robyn, a Rico. It's gray-haired ladies sitting down to a side salad, a bowl of Maryland crab soup, the pork chop special with two vegetables. It's post-shift bus drivers drinking ten-dollar bottles of wine, Johns Hopkins poets ordering another pitcher of Miller Light, dreadlocked white boys drinking something a little nicer. It's Indian graduate students, older round-the-corner men eating late breakfasts, young parents hurrying through early dinners. At the best bar in the world, I've met firefighters, doctors, novelists, community organizers, cops, dudes from Sweden, weed dealers, and a current United States senator. It's older Black couples on dates. It's young gay boys and girls on dates. It's walking canes hung on handrails. It's Baltimore accents for days. In a city that can feel awfully segregated, everyone hangs out there.

The game will be on, and when there's no game, the jukebox isn't bad. There are clear plastic tablecloths, bunches of fake grapes, naughty old matchbooks along the bar's back mirror. There's a fireplace that burns actual wood. The walls are given over to fallen heroes: Michael Jackson, Elvis, Marilyn Monroe, Whitney Houston, David Bowie, Prince. There's a dessert case, within which slowly revolve towering slices of cake. If you have to wait for the bathroom, you dance with the servers rushing into and out of the kitchen. If the *City Paper*, when it was still around, had awarded Most Colorful Cursing, Rico, the server, would have won every year. And it wouldn't have been close.

It's not that the Dizz is stuck in 1970 or 1980, but it's not sprinting, exhausted, overpriced, toward 2020, either. If I had to pick, I'd say the Dizz is somewhere around, let's say, 1994 or maybe 1999 or even 2002, and it has not yet gotten a cell phone, though it's thinking about it; has not consulted with a mixologist because it never will; and has decided that, hey, you there, in the shirt and jeans and sneakers or boots, neck tattoos or not, have a seat wherever, but if you want to order something to eat, do it before 10:30, though they could probably fry you up something after that if you hurry.

Baltimore, as you might have heard, is famous for its poverty and its violence, twin ills that have complex sources but that certainly have to do with the loss of manufacturing jobs and many decades of racial segregation. But it's at the same time a lovely place, a fighting place, a charmer. It's easy to overdo this kind of thing, the bruised fighter with the heart of gold, but clichés are at their cores, truth. Of course, my city's not the only place with two sides. San Francisco both glimmers and stinks. Little Appalachian towns, all rolling hills and fast creeks and twenty-year-old sedans needing muffler work, can delight a spirit but also crush it. It's just that our bruises here in Baltimore are not on the leg but on the face. Absolutely, you come visit and we can see art and theater and listen to symphonies and eat fancy burgers if you want. And then, after that, we'll drink a whole lot of cheap beer, climb up on someone's roof, and set off some fireworks, and if you make it through all of that, I promise you we'll be friends forever.

"We're not like those other cities," a friend once said. He was talking about shinier, richer towns. Towns with more expensive salads. "But we don't want to be."

What I'm saying is that absolutely I'd love fifty more bike lanes. That I'd give a toe if it meant a halving of the number of handguns out there in waistbands, stashed in abandoned doorways. But we've got a few bike lanes, and I've got all my digits. A lot of people—but by no means all of the people—can afford to buy a house here. There's not a lot of pretension. It often takes a full five minutes of conversation before you get asked what you do for a living. And we've got places like the Dizz.

Just after the end of World War II, his corner of the city presumably still rubble, George Orwell wrote for the *Evening Standard* his description of the perfect, idealized London pub, which he thought ought to be called the Moon Under Water.

Orwell had ten criteria, many of them what I can only call exceedingly British, among which were Victorian furnishings, an absence of radios or pianos, cigarettes for sale (sure), aspirins (fair enough), and stamps (drunk letter-writing?), liver-sausage sandwiches and mussels and biscuits with caraway seeds, stout on tap, and, perhaps most importantly, Orwell's perfect pub had to serve beer in handled mugs or, even better, mugs made of china. No London pub, circa 1946, satisfied even nine of his ten criteria. Only a few ticked off eight.

If the Dizz had comment cards, and if you forced me to fill one out, the only thing I'd change would be booths instead of the high-tops along the bar's back wall. I'd adjust the air conditioning from Deep Arctic to merely Pretty Cold.

And that's it. The Dizz isn't for everybody, but of course if it were, it would not be the best bar in the world, or even close. I guess you could call it a dive, but, you know, "dive" to me has always just meant "good bar." The best bar in the world is Kelly and Robyn and Rico, it's Bohs for two-fifty and bags of Utz Party Mix for thirty-five cents (up from a quarter). It's sheets of paper with handwritten specials and it's the Orioles on the big TV, bottom of the ninth, down two, two runners on, the meat of the order up.

One night a couple of springs ago, it was just that: bottom of the ninth, the Os down two, two on, Mark Trumbo up, his big California face huge on the TV, jaw set tight, eyes boring holes into the pitcher.

The best bar in the world shows games of all kinds, but the only ones that really matter are the Ravens and the Orioles. Everybody's nuts for the Ravens, but the Ravens are football and football seems almost too easy to like and also somehow compulsory. The Ravens are a crab cake sandwich, but the Orioles are long talks on the phone until the battery dies, an old, cold dog curled up next to the wood-burning stove. The Orioles are *Moby-Dick*. Stop me if this is all too much. No, don't. The Orioles on the TV at your favorite bar with your friends, in this city that will tackle you and then hand you another beer—that's love.

Because here's the pitch, and we're all there, faces soft in the dimmed Tuesday night lights, all of us up too late but who cares: the federal employee, the chef, the writer, the drummer, the social worker, the guitar player, the young lady who is now my wife, and me.

Trumbo doesn't get hold of that pitch every night, but this night he does, launching that pill into the bullpen, and it's good night, game over, see you tomorrow. And though it's just game number twenty-two or thirty-four or whatever it is out of 162, and though we're not the best team in the league or the prettiest or the richest or anything else, the Dizz erupts, all of us shouting "Trumbo jumbo, Trumbo jumbo, Trumbo jumbo!" and then Kelly or Robyn pours us another pitcher and Rico drops it off, and though the best bar in the world may not be the shiniest, that's exactly the quality that makes it the best, the thing that keeps us here, in this town that takes a little effort to love. Because if you let it in, the Dizz will love you back, and then you're a goner.

Editor's note: As of 2019, the Dizz was a goner as well.

Tara Coxson Crawley's Baltimore Crab Cakes

Ingredients:
2 pounds jumbo lump Maryland crabmeat
¼ cup of panko breadcrumbs or cracker meal
1 cup mayonnaise
2 large eggs
2 tbsp of Old Bay seasoning
1 tbsp of Worcestershire sauce
1 tbsp of lemon juice
5 to 10 drops of hot sauce to taste (optional)

Directions:
In a large bowl, mix together mayonnaise, eggs, Old Bay seasoning, Worcestershire sauce, hot sauce (if preferred) and lemon juice. Set aside.

In another large bowl, put crab meat and gently toss with panko breadcrumbs or cracker meal. Add half of the wet mix to crabmeat and gently fold together. Put the mix in the refrigerator for several hours or overnight.

Form crab cakes into desired size and place on a nonstick baking sheet.

Place in a 375-degree oven for 10 minutes. Remove and finish under the broiler for one to two minutes or until crab cakes are golden brown.

Brooks vs. Cal

CHARLIE VASCELLARO

In a city where athletes playing for professional sports teams are often identified by their first names, two familiar faces and names are most readily associated with the modern-era Baltimore Orioles.

"Brooks" and "Cal."

If you said "Robinson" and asked Orioles fans to fill in the first name, you might get equal parts Frank or Brooks.

Likewise, the surname "Ripken" would elicit three replies spanning two generations: father Cal and sons Junior and Billy. In casual Baltimore parlance, they are simply "Brooks" and "Cal"—you know, like "Earl" and "Boog" and "Eddie."

In the Statue Garden at Oriole Park, there are five slightly larger-than-life sculptures of the five Baltimore Orioles enshrined at the National Baseball Hall of Fame.

The statues were unveiled during the magical return-to-glory season of 2012. They are manager Earl Weaver; Jim Palmer, the franchise's greatest pitcher; 1966 American League MVP and Triple Crown winner Frank Robinson; and switch-hitting slugger Eddie Murray, along with Brooks and Cal.

Of them all, Brooks and Cal are arguably the most iconic and the most revered.

A year before, in October of 2011, a privately commissioned statue of Robinson, depicting the Gold Glove winning third baseman in action, setting his feet and about to throw across the diamond to first base, was unveiled. It stands at the intersection of Russell Street and Washington Boulevard, just across the street from Oriole Park. The public installation basically forced the hand of Orioles owner Peter Angelos to create a similar tribute to the team's Hall of Famers at Oriole Park.

Brooks made his major league debut in September 1955 at the end of the Orioles' second season in the modern era. He appeared in just six games toward the end of the season but would eventually become the team's first nationally recognized star player and the face of the franchise.

Catcher Gus Triandos led the 1955 Os with twelve home runs and sixty-five RBIs; his .277 batting average was also the highest among starters. It can be argued that prior to Robinson's emergence, Triandos was the best player for the Orioles during the fledgling franchise's first few seasons, leading the team in home runs every year from 1955 to 1959 and clubbing a career-high thirty in 1958.

After appearing in the big leagues only briefly during parts of three seasons between 1955 and 1957, Brooks secured the starting position at third base in 1958, and with the exception of one return trip to the minors in 1959, he would hold down the position for the next sixteen Gold Glove award-winning seasons.

Brooks was named to his first of eighteen American League All-Star teams in 1960 and, in very Cal Ripken Jr.-like fashion, ran off a streak of four consecutive seasons without missing a game from 1961 through his AL MVP season of 1964 when he slugged a conspicuous, *pre-steroid-era*, career-high twenty-eight home runs with 118 RBI.

Just kidding . . . the idea of Brooks on steroids or any other performance enhancing drug is equivalent to blasphemy in these parts, where his memory is eternally preserved in its Rockwellian, all-American depiction.

And while hitting for power may not have been Robinson's forte, he could swing a heavy bat (I've held some of his game-used lumber in my hands) with consistent power-alley frequency, eclipsing the twenty-home-run plateau in five other seasons.

His numbers at the plate are good but not great and serve to illuminate how his Hall of Fame career is defined more by his reputation as one of baseball's greatest glove men and perhaps the greatest third baseman of all time.

Brooks's stellar defense played a major role in the greatest six-season run in Orioles franchise history, coinciding with the arrival of Frank (who liked to say that Brookie was his "brother from another mother") Robinson in 1966. It was bolstered by a sturdy and durable pitching staff that included Hall of Famer Jim Palmer and aces like Mike Cuellar and Dave McNally.

But perhaps his greatest contribution and the defining element of his personality is the congenial and benevolent way in which he conducted himself as a ballplayer on and off the field and the way he led his teams by example.

The turning point in the Orioles' fortunes arrived with Frank in 1966 when Baltimore, like the rest of the country, was embroiled in a period of racial turmoil and civil unrest. Frank Robinson was one of a small group of African American players on the team, and Brooks Robinson was acknowledged as the team's leader in the locker room.

In Bob Luke's 2016 book, *Integrating the Orioles,* former Maryland State Delegate Troy Brailey said, "[Brooks] did more to make it easier for them than anyone else."

A young Brooks Robinson at Yankee Stadium.
Credit: Vascellaro Baseball Archives.

Brooks hailed from stringently segregated Little Rock, Arkansas. Upon his arrival in the minor league town of York, Pennsylvania, in 1955, he admitted to "never having competed with or against a Black in my life," with the exception of playground ball as a kid. This did not keep him from being immediately friendly with his few Black teammates in the Orioles organization.

"He was a friend to all of us on the team. Something the Blacks really appreciated in those days," said African American outfielder Dave Pope, who teamed with Robinson for parts of the 1955 and 1956 seasons.

"I suspect Brooks was a key reason why, for the first time in my 14 years of professional baseball, Black players and white players had meals and drinks together when we were on the road," wrote Frank Robinson in his *Extra Innings* book.

Whereas Brooks Robinson's time with the Orioles can best be described as the franchise "Golden Era," the Orioles' fortunes took a different turn during Cal Ripken's twenty-one-year career.

Cal was preceded in the team's lore by his father Cal Ripken Sr., a baseball lifer who spent thirty-six years with the Orioles organization as a minor league player, scout, coach, and manager at the major and minor league levels.

After imbibing his proverbial cup of coffee in twenty big league games in 1981, Cal, or Junior as he was called in the clubhouse, burst onto the big league scene in 1982, knocking twenty-eight home runs with ninety-three RBIs en route to the American League Rookie of the Year Award.

Little did Cal know that he would be playing in the first of his enduring, record-setting 2,632 consecutive games after sitting out the second game of a doubleheader on May 29, 1982. He wouldn't miss either game of a doubleheader or any games on the Orioles schedule until September 20, 1998.

"I don't come to the park and say, 'I'm going to add another game to my streak today.' I come instead to the park saying, 'This is the only game today and I want to play in it,'" Cal told Baltimore baseball writer Ted Patterson.

In the storybook fashion that would become a running theme throughout his career, Cal followed up his rookie of the year campaign with the 1983 AL MVP Award and the Orioles' first World Series since 1970. As of 2021, it was their last.

That year, Cal led the American League in games played (162, of course), plate appearances (726), at bats (663), runs (121), hits (211) and doubles (47) with twenty-seven home runs, eighty-six RBIs, and a .304 batting average. He was also named to the first of nineteen straight All-Star teams.

He must have thought it would be this way forever, but Cal would never play in another World Series game and would only reach the postseason two more times in 1996 and 1997. He was usually the best, or one of the best, players on mostly mediocre and, at times, underachieving teams.

Ripken is the Orioles all-time in games played (3,001), hits (3,184), RBIs (1,695), walks (1,121), at bats (11,551), doubles (603), runs (1,647) total bases (5,168), and home runs (431).

The Orioles compiled a 1,631–1,642 record during Cal Jr's twenty-plus seasons with the club from 1981 to 2001, a .498 winning percentage compared to the team's 1,887–1,461 (.563) record during Brooks's more than twenty-one seasons with the team. excluding his very brief stints in 1955 and 1956.

The Orioles won two World Series (1966, 1970) and four other American League pennants (1969, 1971, 1973, and 1974) during Brooks's time with the club. These icons obviously played during decidedly different eras as far as the business, marketing, and presentation of the game is concerned.

According to BaseballReference.com and the Society for American Baseball Research, Brooks earned a total of $856,000 during his career from 1955 to 1976, topping out at $120,000 for his final season.

Cal Jr. raked in more than $70 million from 1981–2001 and well over twice as much in endorsements.

About a decade into his career with the Orioles, Brooks bought into a restaurant called the Gorsuch House at 511 Gorsuch Avenue at Greenmount, partnering with former big leaguer Eddie Robinson.

"He was in the business by himself since 1960. I joined in 1963. It was only about two minutes away from the ballpark [Memorial Stadium]. Joe Hamper, the old comptroller for the Orioles was the other partner, the three of us were in it for a good while," said Robinson.

Brooks was at a point in his life and career where he felt like investing in the community.

"I was just in to see what happened and make a little money. We sold it around 1970," said Robinson. "We had a nice little restaurant. A lot of the players from different teams stopped over and had dinner after games. We had a nice bar. We even had a Key Club for private events. I'd invite guys like Tom Matte and other guys from the Colts.

"I got married in 1960, I've been with my wife Connie 60 years this October, she was from Canada and Detroit and I was from Little Rock and we weren't going back to any of those places so we decided to stay in Baltimore."

It was a different time when ballplayers lived in the same neighborhoods as working-class fans.

"I had a breakout year in 1960," said Brooks. "I finished third behind Maris and Mantle for the MVP Award and we made a good run at the pennant that year. I lived on Medford Road off Loch Raven Boulevard right across from the Veteran's hospital.

"My wife had never seen the place. It was a row home. I bought it from L. G. Dupre, he played [football] for Baylor and they called him 'Long Gone.' Boog Powell lived two doors down on our street. And I sold it to Dave McNally when I moved out about 1964 and I think he sold it to a hockey player," said Robinson.

The rest of Brooks's story sounds about the same as any middle-class family.

"We went out to Lutherville and lived at 1506 Sheerbrook Road. The only kid we had left was our daughter [Diana]—she was the youngest and when she finished school we decided to sell the house and move into a condominium right across the street from Johns Hopkins University, sold our house, and moved into the Colonnade right across from the lacrosse field," recalled Robinson.

Cal lived famously in a castle surrounded by a moat in an affluent and exclusive suburban neck of the woods known as Worthington Valley near Glyndon. The estate is not really surrounded by a moat, but the sprawling twenty-four acres does contain what looks like a fishing pond, a professional-dimension baseball field, a regulation indoor basketball court, an industrial-size gym, training facilities, and a movie theater.

Like Brooks passing his place along to Dave McNally, Ripken sold the place to former Orioles center fielder Adam Jones in 2018 for $3.46 million, a fraction of the home's original $12.5 million purchase price. Jones later flipped it for $3.55 million.

Cal's presence was in effect more at the ballpark than in the city or any neighborhood, and he was careful to maintain his sparkling image, converting it into a brand. He signed countless autographs, so many that they're devalued on the memorabilia market.

"I sign balls, bats, baseball cards, scorecards, snap-shots and big glossy pictures . . . Wheaties boxes, a million other items, and my favorites—little scraps of paper and smashed popcorn boxes with sneaker prints that can have only one purpose: holding a real memory for someone, maybe for a lifetime," said Ripken in Mike Gesker's *Orioles Encyclopedia*.

Cal had an innate understanding of what his fans and the general public were thinking and feeling.

I witnessed this one night in Cooperstown prior to his Hall of Fame induction. A woman I know was holding one of the "scraps of paper," not much of a baseball fan, but she was caught up in the excitement of the gathering along Main Street as Cal was entering the Hall. He took the piece of paper and before signing it, looked directly into her eyes and asked, "What are you doing here?"

Cal enjoyed a deified, living legend status afforded to only a few players while they're still active. In the wake of the baseball strike of 1994, during which he was fast approaching Lou Gehrig's hallowed record streak, he was called upon by the entire baseball community to "save the game."

Though Orioles fans placed him on a pedestal, they never felt the intimacy and near family familiarity they enjoy with Brooks to this day.

In an informal social media poll, Brooks was the fan favorite by a landslide, especially among those who identified as Orioles fans. Those who chose Cal were more likely to be fans of teams from other cities, attesting to Cal's national branding and image.

There is a well-known quote associated with Brooks that best sums up his relationship with the city of Baltimore.

Associated Press baseball writer Gordon Beard was at the podium at a farewell Brooks event toward the end of Robinson's career. Beard, who died in 2009 at age eighty-two, referenced a recently manufactured candy bar named for New York Yankees World Series hero Reggie Jackson.

"Around here, nobody's named a candy bar after Brooks Robinson," said Beard. "We name our children after him."

The Enemies of Beaktown

MIKE RICIGLIANO

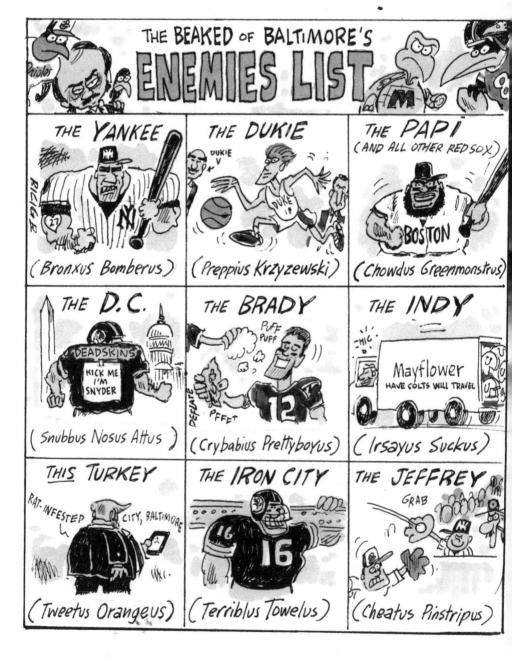

Blue Horseshoes

DEAN BARTOLI SMITH

On a Sunday morning in Baltimore—January 6, 2013—there was a light breeze and temperatures approached fifty degrees under a cloudless blue sky. I turned on my radio to listen to the pregame show while getting dressed for a Ravens playoff game against the Indianapolis Colts.

The somber keys of a piano played, interspersed with the voice of Ray Lewis. "I talked to my team today—about life. Everything that starts has an end. I told my team this would be my last ride," he said, fighting back tears.

The news of Ray's retirement was only five days old, and the weight of it hit me. Tears welled in my eyes. This would be the last time I would see number fifty-two playing football at Ravens' stadium. The team was about to face the Indianapolis Colts in a playoff game for the first time since 2006, when Peyton Manning and the Colts had ruined one of the best seasons in Ravens history.

The Ravens had posted a 13–3 record that year, and the city believed victory against the team that had left Baltimore in the middle of the night two decades earlier was all but guaranteed.

The Ravens defense frustrated Peyton Manning by intercepting two passes and keeping the Colts from the end zone, but the Indy defense picked off quarterback Steve McNair twice and prevented the Ravens from scoring. The offense never recovered from a costly interception thrown from the Colts' three-yard line.

Indianapolis won 15–6, and Manning led them to their first Super Bowl victory.

In 2013, the Colts had risen from the ashes of a disastrous 2–14 season in 2011 to finish 11–5 in 2012. Rookie quarterback Andrew Luck passed for twenty-three touchdowns and more than 4,300 yards. With veteran receiver Reggie Wayne and newcomer T. Y. Hilton running routes, Luck engineered a dangerous passing attack. And he had an amazing knack for converting third and long situations by using his quick feet and overall athleticism.

Luck's performance began to fade Indy fans' memories of Peyton Manning, who had moved on to Denver and had led the Broncos to the best record in the AFC. The pundits who picked the Colts over the Ravens in the wild-card game relished the thought of watching Manning duel against Luck in the following week's divisional round in the Rocky Mountains.

"The thing about Luck is, that dude's not normal," said Ravens strong safety Bernard Pollard. "I think [it's] just the type of player that he is, the guy stays calm all game long."

Luck spent the first part of his childhood in London and Frankfurt and is an ardent follower of the Arsenal football club. He didn't start playing American football until the seventh grade in Texas.

The Colts also had a fiery new leader in head coach Chuck Pagano, the Ravens' defensive coordinator in 2011. Pagano had recruited Ed Reed to play at the University of Miami and maintained strong friendships with several Ravens players.

Pagano had taken over for Jim Caldwell, the former head coach of Indy who was now a member of the Ravens' coaching staff and who had just been promoted to offensive coordinator after the late-season dismissal of Cam Cameron.

Diagnosed in September 2012 with acute promyelocytic leukemia, Pagano took indefinite leave from his coaching. Offensive coordinator Bruce Arians assumed head coaching responsibilities while Pagano received treatment.

The football media had billed 2012 as a rebuilding one for Indianapolis; the upstart Colts weren't picked to contend for a playoff spot. But with Pagano watching from a hospital bed, the Colts responded.

Galvanized by their coach's illness, they began winning games. After starting the season 2–3, they won the next nine of eleven to make the playoffs, beating quality teams such as Minnesota, Green Bay, and Houston—a team that had crushed the Ravens in the fifth game of the season. After beating Miami, the Colts received a visit from Pagano, who had left the hospital to be with his team. He told the players they were already champions for defying the preseason predictions for a last-place finish. He went on to say, "My vision that I'm living, is to see two more daughters getting married, dancing at their weddings, and then hoisting that Lombardi several times and watching that confetti fall."

Pagano rejoined the team on the sidelines for the regular season finale against Houston.

The team's motto, "Chuckstrong," served as a potent rallying cry.

On the Wednesday before the Colts game, Ray Lewis announced his retirement from the NFL at the end of the season. He said, choking up, "This is my last ride." Local radio stations in Baltimore celebrated one of the greatest football players of all time and the face of the Ravens franchise since its move to Baltimore in 1996. One caller shared that he had once asked Ray Lewis at a banquet why he wore number fifty-two, and the linebacker told him that it was based on a deck of playing cards.

As a young boy without a father, Lewis had explained, he would pull out a card and do that number of pushups. "It wasn't football that drove me to train," Lewis said in an NFL Films documentary about his life. "It was to stop my mother from coming home with bruises and black eyes."

In Baltimore, the Ray Lewis retirement eclipsed all other stories related to the game, including Pagano's recovery from leukemia. Focused on the legendary middle linebacker, I found it difficult to dredge up what felt like ancient Colts baggage. It was the first time I had personally seen the blue horseshoe against a pure white helmet in a playoff game since Christmas Eve in 1977 when the Raiders came to town. I went with my uncle that night and watched in agony as Oakland won a thrilling double-overtime game.

Now, in 2012, the Colts had become just another team on a glorious playoff afternoon. There were no middle fingers extended to the visiting team bus when it rolled into the lot, as had happened in 2006. I couldn't muster any of the old resentments against a team that had risen above the adversity of having a coach with a life-threatening illness.

Still, former Baltimore Colts linebacker and Ravens announcer Stan White offered his own perspective on the game. "The revenge game was in 2006," he said, "and Chuck is a likable guy. Andrew Luck is likable. They had such a bad season the year before. I didn't hear too much talk about 1984, but I still can't get past the blue horseshoes."

Fans sporting vintage Johnny Unitas jerseys intermingled with Indianapolis Colts fans clad in the numbers of Luck and Manning.

The immaculate sky over M&T Bank Stadium filled with boundless possibilities. I wondered what it would take from the Colts or any team to get Ray Lewis off the field for good. The retirement was certain to elevate the play of his teammates, but what effect would it have on the Indy Colts?

A new season began on the way to the stadium. A sense of gratitude hung in the air. We were gathering to say goodbye to the franchise's iconic player. There would be plenty of time to sift through the body of work after the season, including the complexities of a flawed superstar, but the final home game was about a football player trying to extend his season. The convincing Ravens victory over the New York Giants two weeks before had gone a long way to reinvigorating a skeptical fan base—but the game itself, in some sense, had taken a back seat to Lewis.

More than 71,000 made the pilgrimage, from all around the Baltimore area and beyond, to see Ray Lewis play one last time in person, including

Sheila "Pickles" Miller from the Eastern Shore and her daughter Emily. Pickles didn't know where the stadium was and asked me for directions as we were leaving the parking lot. I pointed out Poe's grave and Babe Ruth's house along the way.

She explained her attendance this way: "I had to see Ray's last game," she said. "We went online this morning and got tickets."

It was miraculous that Lewis was able to play after what had been billed as a season-ending torn right tricep in mid-October. Lewis recalled his phone call with Ozzie Newsome shortly after the injury. "Don't put me on injured reserve," he had asked Newsome. "[Ozzie] was like, 'What do you mean?'" Lewis had replied, "Trust me, I will be back."

Today he wore a contraption that encased his right arm like a knee brace. The star linebacker had lost a step in recent years and was considered a liability against the pass, especially on third down. But after seventeen seasons, he was still better than most players at his position.

He, along with defensive costars Suggs, Lewis, Ellerbe, Pollard, and Ngata, had missed games during the season. Healthy and rested for the first time, the starting defense now stood at the edge of the tunnel, ready to take the field. The ominous pounding chords of Eminem's "Lose Yourself" launched the introductions, and the Ravens' "red eyes" appeared on the Jumbotron.

Announcer Bruce Cunningham belted out the names of the defensive unit. Ed Reed strolled onto the field before Lewis, shaking his head with a finger to his lips as the crowd thundered its customary "Reed!" for several seconds.

Many in the capacity crowd pondered Reed's future with the team. Staying in the moment, he pointed back to the smoking tunnel in an attempt to quiet the crowd and keep the focus on his good friend. Lewis had fallen to his knees in prayer before his name was called.

Then he appeared, his eyes blackened like Marlon Brando's Kurtz from *Apocalypse Now*. His famed "squirrel dance" had one more scheduled run for the hometown crowd. Dirt flew from a chunk of sod. He sashayed from side to side, thrust out his massive torso, and cawed like a Raven.

The Blue Angels roared overhead at the end of the national anthem. He embraced NFL Commissioner Roger Goodell on the Ravens' sideline. We knew as Ravens fans that it would never be like this again. Then Lewis gathered his team around him for one last pregame war party, a ritual he popularized around the NFL. "What time is it? Game Time! What time is it? Game Time!"

The Colts went three and out on their first drive and punted. The Ravens drove to the Colts' eleven-yard line before Ray Rice fumbled—his first of two on that day, and his first of the 2012 season. From the outset, offensive coordinator Jim Caldwell worked the Colts defense laterally.

He moved them from side to side, progressing gradually down the field. Rice ran off tackle left for three yards. Flacco passed right to Ed Dickson for twenty-four yards. Rice ran left for four yards. But nothing was sustained, and the teams traded possessions in a scoreless first quarter.

Using an assortment of slants and quick outs, the Colts drove to the Ravens' thirty-yard line early in the second quarter. Luck's quick release was faster than any I had ever seen. He barely took two steps before rifling the ball out, and the Colts receivers were difficult to defend on five- and seven-yard patterns. Former Pittsburgh offensive coordinator Arians had developed a game plan that was the exact replica of past Steelers games, with quick outs to the wide receivers and pick plays right off the line of scrimmage. (In a strange twist, Arians himself had come down with an undisclosed illness and was watching from the hospital.) The drive came to an abrupt end when linebacker Paul Kruger sacked Luck, causing a fumble that was recovered by Raven Pernell McPhee. McPhee carried the ball off the field and presented it to Ray Lewis as if to say, "Take this ball, I just did this for you." The retirement announcement was paying off as a motivational tool for the younger players. "We made a commitment to each other," Lewis would say after the game.

Running back Bernard Pierce put the offense on his back to begin the second quarter and rumbled into field goal range with thirty-one yards on four carries. The rookie from Temple would finish with 103 yards on thirteen carries. Justin Tucker's foot edged the Ravens into the lead 3–0.

Luck almost threw a pick-six to Ray Lewis on the Colts' next possession. With the field in a mix of sun and shadow, the ball landed in Lewis's hands, and he tipped it up into his helmet, then deflected it again before it fell harmlessly to the turf. The play would have resulted in a touchdown for the Ravens and was eerily reminiscent of two tipped Manning passes in the 2006 playoff game that should have been intercepted.

The Ravens scored their first touchdown following a forty-seven-yard screen pass to Ray Rice that ended at the two-yard line. He caught the ball in a crowd of defenders and darted through a seam down the right sideline. Flacco targeted two passes to seldom-used receiver Tandon Doss in the end zone, and they both fell incomplete. But Vonta Leach bulled his way in from the two and the Ravens led 10–3. On third and twenty-six from the Colts' forty-one with twenty-nine seconds left in the half, Luck dropped back to pass. Under pressure, he raced up through the pocket to the line of scrimmage and uncorked a perfect strike to T. Y. Hilton for a first down in Ravens territory. He threw the ball from right to left across the field on a rope. It resembled a play that a seasoned Fran Tarkenton would have made for the Minnesota Vikings. Luck simply knew where his receivers were going to be on the field, and he created a few extra seconds to locate Hilton. Adam Vinatieri kicked a fifty-two-yard field goal, and the Colts trailed 10–6 at half. It was scary to watch how quickly Luck could move his team into scoring position. Jim Caldwell was calling his fourth game as the new Ravens offensive coordinator. After a 34–17 home loss to Denver, his efforts against the New York Giants had produced a 33–14 blowout. The season-ending loss to the Bengals was played more like a preseason affair and didn't really count, as many key players were allowed to rest.

Now Caldwell's leadership skills were needed again, and he appeared to relax Joe Flacco and give him confidence. The ex-head coach had his own motivation, too. He had taken the Colts to the Super Bowl in 2009 but lost to the Saints. He still had something to prove against his former team. The offense had begun to buy in over the last couple of weeks. Caldwell's protection schemes were more robust than Cameron's and didn't leave Flacco exposed as much. Cameron had liked to use an empty backfield formation that telegraphed to everyone in the stadium that the Ravens were going to pass.

The offensive line had also been retooled, with Bryant McKinnie being released from his season-long "doghouse" status to play left tackle. He had shown up to camp out of shape after promising that he would be ready. His slow gait getting to the line did not mesh well with the no-huddle offense Cameron had employed. He had played so well in practice that Ed Reed had been yelling, "Bring back B-Mac." But that was in the past now, and writers like Mike Preston of the *Baltimore Sun*, who had been calling for this change to happen, finally got their wish. Michael Oher moved to right tackle and rookie Kelechi Osemele went to left guard. It worked. The Colts only sacked Flacco once, and the reengineered line neutralized Colts defensive stalwarts Robert Mathis and Dwight Freeney.

This structural improvement helped change the complexion of the postseason, giving Joe Flacco the few extra seconds he needed to make plays. In the locker room at halftime, one player voiced his frustration that the play calling had been too conservative. Receiver Anquan Boldin hadn't caught a pass the entire half, and he was seething. The Ravens would later say that they had wanted to see what the Colts were going to do in the first half before opening up the offense. With Pagano on the far sideline, it was a fair point. He had intimate knowledge of the Ravens' playbook, having served as defensive coordinator. The coaches understood Boldin's frustration. "They listened because he's not a complainer," said football commentator Syreeta Hubbard of theNFLchick.com. "He is a leader and his words were taken seriously."

The veteran receiver who had joined the Ravens prior to the 2010 season to win a Super Bowl had been lost at times in Cameron's offensive schemes over the past three years. Cameron often treated Boldin as a last resort and didn't believe he could get separation from his defenders. "Boldin is never open," Cameron had told the coaching staff in response to why the receiver's number wasn't called more often, according to those close to the team. Anquan didn't fit with the flash and speed of the no-huddle offense and had trouble gaining separation. He performed the role of possession receiver on a team with speedy wideouts Jacoby Jones and Torrey Smith. For the past two seasons, the Ravens had resorted to number eighty-one only when the game was on the line and they needed a score.

The Ravens received the second half kickoff and started play from their own eighteen-yard line. On the second play from scrimmage, Robert Mathis sacked Joe Flacco for a thirteen-yard loss. On the next play, Flacco dropped back to pass. He rolled right, pursued by Colts defenders, and stopped short of the Colts' sideline. It looked like he was going to throw the ball away and run out of bounds, but he launched a fifty-yard bomb down the far sideline to Boldin, who beat Antoine Bethea and made the catch at the Colts' forty-one. It looked like a desperation Hail Mary, but it was not. A similar "scramble play" had been called for Torrey Smith in the Ravens' loss to the Patriots one year before; that ball was underthrown or the play would have led to a touchdown. This year, the play unveiled an aggressive, risk-taking approach that had been missing all year.

On their next drive, Flacco found Boldin again for a forty-six-yard strike down the sideline. It was a beautiful, big-armed Flacco pass—perfectly timed and placed into Boldin's hands. Then Flacco hit Dennis Pitta on a crossing pattern for a twenty-yard touchdown pass to take a 17–6 lead with eight minutes remaining in the third. The Colts stormed back, attacking the middle of the Ravens defense with short passes. At thirty-seven, Lewis could still play the run, but he struggled against the pass, and offenses around the league finally had a way to beat him. Luck drove the Colts seventy-one yards before the drive fizzled at the Ravens' nine. The Baltimore defense stood its ground, denying the Colts six points again, but Adam Vinatieri kicked a field goal to keep Indy within a touchdown and a two-point conversion at 17–9.

To start the fourth quarter, the Ravens sprung Ray Rice for an eighteen-yard run, but the ball was punched out from under his arm with a blindside hit, and the Colts recovered on their own twenty-nine. Andrew Luck began a drive into Ravens territory by connecting with Reggie Wayne for nineteen yards, and then running back Vick Ballard broke off a twenty-four-yard run. Then the Ravens' "red zone" defense stiffened again. The Rice fumble had no repercussions as Vinatieri missed a forty-yard field goal wide. On the next series, Pierce broke free for a forty-three-yard gain. In a contrast of running styles, where Ray Rice slammed head-on into a hole whether it was there or not, Pierce on this play held back until his blocking fell into place, and the big runner with deceptive and explosive speed blasted through the hole toward the end zone.

Then Flacco called Boldin's number again. Covered by Darius Butler, Boldin gained a half step in the right corner of the end zone. Flacco saw the one-on-one coverage and lofted a pass high and toward the back corner. Butler defended it perfectly, thrusting his right arm into Boldin's chest as the ball arrived. But blessed with vise grips for hands, Boldin locked onto the ball and Butler's arm as both players crashed to the end zone turf.

One photo angle showed Boldin's eyes fixed on the ball in his hands a full head and shoulders above Butler's hand. The receiver with the mindset of a linebacker had elevated his game. Boldin caught the touchdown pass with a vengeance that suggested he would come down with the ball by any means necessary, even if he had to take the defender's arm with him. With his fifth and final reception of the game, Boldin had racked up 145 receiving yards, a new Ravens playoff record for a wide receiver.

This brilliant touchdown catch sent a message to his quarterback and to his team that he would catch any ball thrown near him. At the Ravens' postgame press conference, it came out that Boldin had approached Joe Flacco before the game and told him he felt like he had 200 yards in him. "I just wanted to go out and give everything. I think everyone in the locker room wanted to make sure this wasn't our last game. I think we all have a goal in mind, and we're focused in on that goal."

With five minutes remaining, Cary Williams sealed the victory by intercepting Luck. As the Ravens ran out the clock, Lewis came in for the final play, and Flacco was honored to have him in the backfield. Ray tossed in a bonus squirrel dance that miffed Colt Reggie Wayne. Then he took a victory lap around the stadium á la Orioles star Cal Ripken's tour after breaking Lou Gehrig's record for consecutive games played.

The Ravens had won a hard-fought game 24–9. It wasn't a work of art by any means. They battled and broke a few big plays downfield, and at other times, they struggled. Nineteen games in and they still hadn't put together sixty minutes of football. They had beaten the Giants soundly two weeks prior by putting up twenty-four points in the first half but only nine in the second half. Flacco had arguably played his best game of the year that day, but they could improve upon a few things, like goal line offense, that would come in handy in the playoffs.

The Colts' offense had run them ragged everywhere but the end zone, but the Ravens' defense continued to uphold its stingy "bend don't break" mantra inside the red zone, and their veteran effort harkened back to the 2000 Super Bowl team and a record-breaking defense that only gave up 165 points all season.

That team held opponents without touchdowns for long stretches. Lewis had played an integral role back then, defending both the pass and run with an unbridled fury. He finished this game with thirteen tackles— and a clear vulnerability to the pass.

The Colts amassed 419 yards, but they didn't score a touchdown. They ran a mind-boggling eighty-seven plays in the game, keeping the Ravens' defense on the field for thirty-seven minutes. With Peyton Manning waiting in the wings for the Ravens on the following Saturday in Denver, the prognosticators believed that the former Colt would carve up the Ravens' defense and pass for several touchdowns.

Lewis mentioned that he had already turned his iPad in to receive Denver game film because "it's on to the next one." After the game, Ravens coach John Harbaugh addressed Ray Lewis, Chuck Pagano, and the city's relationship to its former team. "I think we're grateful for the opportunity to be here and to witness this historic moment in sports," said Harbaugh. "It seems like [Lewis] played really well. And, it wasn't just about one guy. Nobody understands it more than the one guy we're talking about. It was about a team. It was about a city."

This playoff game will be remembered as the moment the lingering Colts' abandonment issues went away for good. "That was thirty years ago," said Michael Olesker, the author of *The Colts' Baltimore*, referring to the loss of the team in 1984. The only Baltimore professional football player to come close to matching the impact that the great Johnny Unitas had on his team and his city had just played his last down at home.

The sports talk shows had already chiseled Lewis's visage into a hypothetical "Mount Rushmore of Baltimore Sports" that included Unitas, Brooks Robinson, and Cal Ripken. Lewis had earned his place next to them.

Ode to Lucille Clifton

JACKIE OLDHAM

She lived an ordinary life—
Wife, mother,
Government worker, Teacher,
Essayist, and Poet

Revealing, through her writing,
Her extraordinary inner life

Of trauma and healing,
pain and joy,
Injustice and paradox.

In language
Plain and simple,

She detailed Truth and History,

With grace and humor,
Wit,
Infused with mystery.

All hallmarks
Of the Human Condition,

Personal and temporal

In the Universe eternal.

Lucille Clifton (1936–2010) was awarded the Lannan Literary Award for Poetry in 1996.
Credit: Jennifer Bishop.

Fitzgerald and Baltimore

DAN MALONEY

In 1935, F. Scott Fitzgerald noted of his new home in Baltimore, "I belong here, where everything is civilized and gay and rotted and polite."

Nearly ninety years later, I share both Fitzgerald's gin-riddled admiration of the city and his status here as an outsider. For a city of people where everyone seems to have known everyone else (and their family and their high school) forever, I too am a stranger in a strange land: a suburban Philadelphian in downtown Baltimore.

At least Fitzgerald had his great uncle: the Francis Scott Key of "Oh Say Can You See" fame. I can barely find a slice of decent pizza that would be passable in Philadelphia, let alone an ancestral relative. Still, the English teacher in me—the one who gets into debates about the mastery of *Tender is the Night*—is always eager for any connection to Scott.

Fitzgerald wrote *Tender is the Night*, published 1934, in Baltimore.

With an English teacher's reverence, I reflected on Fitzgerald's quote deeply—how his descriptors have changed, shifted—but how they ultimately seem remarkably accurate for Baltimore.

As I wander through the neighborhood of Mount Vernon—the historic artistic and queer heart of the city—past the grave of Fitzgerald's ancestor at the Methodist church, or the gorgeous Walters Art Museum with its remarkable collection of antiquities, or my favorite watering hole, Stable and Saloon—Baltimore's gayness, politeness, and sense of belonging shine through (though perhaps not in all the ways that Fitzgerald initially intended).

More often than not, it can appear that Baltimore is as rotted as Fitzgerald described it a lifetime ago. Surrounded by the urban decay of many of America's East Coast cities, Baltimore batters on, demeaned by presidential rants, ravaged by gun violence and addiction, haunted by racial prejudice. At times—even among the most optimistic apologists of the city against the suburban naysayers—one can get down on the city and question how much charm possibly endures in Charm City.

And yet—as Fitzgerald writes in *Gatsby*, that great American novel that is the essential workhorse of American literary curricula, and which I teach at an all-boys school north of the city, "Life starts all over again when it gets crisp in the fall."

Though for me, my renewed opinion about Baltimore started in the fall, outside the city—out in the county, at a state park no less. Leave it to nature to renew the griping urbanite.

When I drove out to Patapsco State Park, I had many thoughts about "Baltimore rot" and much less about its warmth and possibility. But at Patapsco, I felt much more confident about the future.

I first visited Patapsco on a Labor Day weekend, traditionally viewed as the end of summer and the last hurrah of shore-goers everywhere.

For a teacher, Labor Day is a monumental transition. On one side is the illusionary relaxation of having the summer off; on the other, next year's crop of students who are ravenous for your time and energy.

In between was Patapsco State Park—the first in Maryland—and I was struck by its serene beauty. That morning, the air was slightly damp, without a chill, and the summer green had not yet begun to fade.

In the deepest parts of the trail, when the quiet is only interrupted by an occasional crack of a branch or running water, it is easy to muse poetically about an existence free of the cares beyond the parking lot.

Patapsco covers such a vast space that it seems hard to believe—once you're in the midst of it—that you're surrounded by suburban sprawl, just half an hour from the city of Baltimore. Aren't the moments alone in the heart of nature what holiday weekends are for?

Of course, at a state park on a holiday weekend, these sublime moments are few, and the trail was packed with other hikers. Rather than stir my deepest social outrage, the crowd inspired me. It allowed me to see the rich, unrotted life of Baltimore, and I was heartened.

Because, despite it all, life in Baltimore is wonderfully rich. Several years ago, the *Baltimore Sun* identified a handful of communities in the city worthy of the title "global neighborhoods." This was because they lacked a dominant ethnic majority and embraced the mixing of cultures.

On the day of my hike, it felt as though Patapsco State Park was also another global neighborhood.

Everywhere were voices from around the world, no doubt considering whether one should turn back, asking if anyone had a snack; all engaged, as I was, in the great outdoors. At Patapsco, I observed and joined residents of all ages, ethnic backgrounds, and genders. They walked alone or with families—kids and nieces and godchildren and babies slung in papooses.

There were people with leashed dogs, and overstuffed backpacks, and ill-advised shoes. At one juncture, I made way for four hikers as they carried a friend who had injured her ankle on the journey.

The visit to Patapsco gave me hope for the future. It reminded me of yet another Fitzgerald quote: "Baltimore is warm, but pleasant—I love it more than I thought."

I love it much more than I thought as well. Perhaps the worst is behind us if we follow the ultimate Fitzgerald direction: We must beat on.

Pratt Street & I

FERNANDO QUIJANO III

This is Pratt Street, & I
walk it alone, sidewalks empty
of my childhood—the *bodega*
where we picked penny candies
using discarded couch
coins on our way to school,
walked Willow to the dopplered
sounds of Salsa beats blaring by,
by the saintly scents of the *botanica*
where the *orisha* hid
behind Catholic masks praying
to gods long abandoned,
forgotten,
forlorn.

This is Pratt Street, & I
walk it alone, from 2031
to Hampstead Hill,
a shoe factory
excuse for a school
where black fights white
near twin octopi
in the valley
of Patterson Park
every Friday—
part of some neverending race
riot ritual that amounts to pushes
& shoves & not much else.
I'm asked to choose
sides; but how do I
pick a fight that's not mine?

This is Pratt Street, & I
walk it alone, across the vast
expanse of Patterson Park,
past an out of place pagoda
sitting atop a hill I hear
blasted British ships from high
cannons—Hampstead Hill, the real
one, not its namesake school
I feel doomed
to attend, where last
week a kid lit a fire
in a trashcan, sending
the Hungarian French teacher
to Sheppard Pratt,
Baltimore's Bellevue
in my view.

This is Pratt Street, & I
walk it alone, past a boat lake
without boats, rainhouses
protecting young lovers
hidden in the shadows
of its iron archways held
together by rivets
the size of my fists, basketball
courts full of netless rims,
8811 sipping
coffee in his patrol
car until he feels
ready to emerge
just to harass middle
schoolers for whom he holds
particular unwarranted antipathy,
& past those damned octopi—
upon one's back I kissed a girl
who dumped me the next
day because I was too short,
or too dark,
or too both.

This is Pratt Street, & I
walk it alone every Saturday
past Obrycki's, always flanked
by limos & smelling of old bay,
to Broadway by two to get to
the only Hispanic store I knew,
open that one day, only until four,
to pick up some *Sazon, recao,*
plátanos, y guayaba for *mami*
to earn my *malta* that I will down
ice cold between Bank & Gough
& be briefly tasted back to Hoboken,
home again, until it wasn't.

This is Pratt Street, & I
walk it alone every summer
for one weekend in June
when Fells Point transforms
into a chimera—a fusion
of sounds & scents & accents
reminiscent of my childhood,
but muddied by the blend
of cultures sharing nothing
with me but a language,
until eight when the sun drops
low in the horizon & Salsa fills
the air—congas laying rhythms
that carry the weight of blowing
horns, colored by the calling
chorus & the response cutting
through it all from the dulcet
voice of *el cantante,*
& I get lost in the crowd
of dancers flipping their hips
& spinning, & I close
my eyes, letting it all
wash over me like a Caribbean
wave & I twirl & finally find
myself,
home.

South Chapel Street

CHRISTOPHER MCNALLY

The first thing I noticed about the home was its painted screens, lovely pastoral painted screens. And Formstone—the kind with the pink and gray stones. My Uncle Bill, who bought the house as an investment, offered it to me for $400.00 a month—perfect for my Sallie-Mae-law-school-student-loan budget. Big enough for a roommate if they were under five feet ten inches tall and could fit into the third-floor pitched roof bedroom (more of an attic with a small dormer window that barely would accommodate a small air conditioner).

The house had no heat aside from a brown, gas-fed box in the kitchen with a metal chimney that snaked its way to the ceiling. It was built as slave quarters, Uncle Bill said. This house had a sidewalk in front that was perhaps three feet wide and a small brick stoop—just big enough for that great Baltimore pastime of stoop sitting. No central air—but luckily, I had a whole truckful of my late grandmother's furniture, having raided her home in Cape May, New Jersey, just a month before. She had died earlier that year following a long battle with lung cancer. I would furnish this place as I remembered her living room—paisley couch, leaded crystal lamps, and a Formica table. I had her china, dishes, air-conditioners, even her vacuum. And her seventy-eight records but nothing to play them on.

Fells Point! The street was colorful. Star Alley they once called it. I have found this alley on one of the oldest maps of Baltimore. This was 1996. Gentrification had not yet reached the 500 block. Most of the residents were long-time folks who had been there forever. An interracial couple lived across the street and kept to themselves—referred to by the matriarch "Miss Thelma" as "salt and pepper"—probably the most sensitive way she could muster a description of this union. Miss Thelma sat on her folding chair every evening when the temperature was above sixty-five degrees. Her husband—Mr. Joe—could barely walk and sat inside, watching TV all day. Retired from Allied Chemical—as I moved to the house, the EPA was overseeing the largest toxic cleanup from this same plant where Mr. Joe had worked, and the impact on his health was evident the moment you met him. Their daughter was an attractive blond, born-again Christian who married a physician, moved to rural Virginia, away from the evils and sin of the city, and every time she visited her four kids, she practically ran into the house. She was pregnant at sixteen but found Jesus and a good life outside the Holy Land and hated coming back.

But Miss Thelma refused to move from her Civil War-era "eyebrow" three-story row house that probably dated to the Civil War. The granddaughters begged her to accept Jesus as they did not want their grandmother to go to hell, as they had been likely told by their pastor and parents. They had to start their mission right there on S. Chapel Street. Miss Thelma wrote a letter accepting Jesus that was read at her funeral. I knew better. I knew Miss Thelma had written that letter for her granddaughters; she never once set foot in church in the five years I lived there. But she was as good and decent as anyone who did. Jesus loved her no matter what she wrote in a letter. And I loved her for giving her granddaughters the peace that their church had taken from them. Miss Thelma—always a smile and a kind word even though her marriage was loveless and she despised her husband. He had a chance to move into the big house around the corner on Fleet—he refused. Instead, they got Formstone and aluminum awnings to keep the sun out. The house faced west—bad sun in the afternoon. She proudly boasted that she bought the Formstone that was on her house. They moved there in 1959. Back then, the boxcars lined Fleet Street and the slack taken up by the train would cause a loud "barn." She had a circular fluorescent light in her kitchen.

The staircases were all narrow and twisted—anything bigger than a double bed would not even make the turn. I had to build my own box spring out of lumber and plywood from the Home Depot at Eastern and Kane, the last stop for all of the laid-off Sparrows Point workers. These were people that knew how to make bridge steel and were now cutting keys and mixing paint.

Window unit air-conditioners were the only thing that made the house survivable during the summer months. No dishwasher. Small portable apartment washer and dryer. Small fridge. No cable. Many mice. Constantly killing mice.

Other residents included Miss Eva next door. Her back window had a bumper sticker that read "Contribute to your local sex fund." Miss Thelma grumbled that Miss Eva had taken up with the "Samoan" over at Broadway and commented that they used to practically "do it" in the street. The fruit of their union—her son Junior—had just returned from prison, where his two front teeth had been knocked out by a Black guy, he told me. He proudly boasted how nice his teeth used to look. He was unemployable and would be headed back to prison soon. Miss Thelma once commented about Junior "I never liked that boy . . . ever since he was a kid and came over and dropped his pants and took a piss on my wall I never liked him after that." He and his ex-con friends were all living in this nine-foot-wide, 650-square-foot home and used to fish the squalid waters of the Patapsco River at the Canton waterfront for subsistence. Junior used to often ask me if he could use my grill for his fish.

He used to grin a toothless grin and call me his "lawyer." I didn't have the heart to tell him I was only an unlicensed law student. I also never refused his request for use of my grill, thinking that to do so could end badly for me. The first time I met Eva on the day I moved in—while the house was being bombed for the massive infestation of roaches and fleas—I discovered within the first five minutes of living there that she was in her backyard smoking a cigarette. I introduced myself. She turned to me and said between puffs of smoke, "Oh, yeah . . . well, I own this shithole." I said, "oh . . ." She then proceeded to say that her "motherfucking kids trashed the place." Once, I had to call the police after Junior started chasing his small nephew around the house. The police showed up and after they left, Junior burst into the street, banging on every door, wanting to know who had called the police. I hid behind the couch with the lights off.

On the other side—521—lived a prostitute named Rose. She was about sixty years old and smoked weed. Her house looked like a brothel. She had a pimp who drove a Caddy. One day, Rose disappeared. The pimp's buddies moved in and eventually were evicted. Section 8. Next to Rose was Ms. Evelyn and her Hispanic boyfriend. They had a beautiful daughter who did not stand a chance. Her boyfriend's 1969 Oldsmobile had no seat belt, and there was a large gash in the windshield where the daughter's head had struck during an accident.

She seemed okay. One day, Evelyn threw her boyfriend out by tossing drawers full of his clothes into the street, screaming, "Come get your rags, bitch."

Blocked traffic until the police showed up, back when they drove Caprices and had blue light bars on top. SE District.

Next to Evelyn was "the Judge"—his house was completely run-down, yet he used to obsessively repoint his brick every day and talk loudly to himself. He relived a courtroom drama every day, and his comments were laced with pleas to a judge to do something, though it was hard to understand him. He was harmless but unnerving.

Across the street was Travis. He was a Black man who seemed to hate Black people. Raised in Roland Park, his mother was a domestic. He played with white kids and loved heavy metal. He was addicted to drugs and was often drunk.

He had a loud, happy laugh and would play loud music and sing at the top of his lungs. His house should have been condemned. First floor was ripped out to studs. No hot water. The second floor had a bare lightbulb and visible joists. He repaired appliances there with a friend in a white van. They would show up during the day, unload the appliances, repair them, and then leave. He wore Metallica shirts. Played guitar. Did lots of drugs. Harmless and funny.

Tochterman's Fishing and Tackle—the oldest fishing and tackle store in the world—was just up the block at the corner of Eastern and S. Chapel. Tony Tochterman and his girlfriend, Dee, were neighborhood anchors. I wrote an article about their store for the neighborhood newsletter, which I edited—the Mid-Point Association. His store still had the massive glass entrance doors that were probably installed in the 1930s.

A big neon sign with a jumping fish. Rows and rows of fishing rods and every accessory you could possibly imagine. Tony used to complain about the maintenance on the neon sign as it was constantly breaking—he would still get it fixed, always—it was rarely dark. Many days I would sit in my living room and suddenly, a few feet from my window would appear a customer testing a fly-fishing rod, right in the middle of the street. I used to love watching them fly fish in the middle of 500 South Chapel.

Directly behind me was the rear yard of Ostrowski's—the wonderful Polish sausage store that had been there forever. All of the old ladies used to get their Easter sausage on Good Friday and have it blessed by the priest. The neighborhood was once Polish, they said. Holy Rosary on Chester Street still had mass in Polish. I could open my rear window (also my fire escape) and smell the scent of fresh smoked sausage, and it was wonderful. The front window would bring in the scent of Paterakas's bakery—all of the bread for McDonald's up and down the Eastern Seaboard was made down the street in Fells Point—Aliceanna and Caroline St. The bakery factory store on Fleet sold bread for fifty cents per bag.

Fleet Street was a hodgepodge of storefronts that had somehow survived. Siemecks market (great fresh-cut pork chops). Milton Buck appliance—an art deco front with an old man in the window with a handful of gas appliances and a GE neon sign. It was closed by 1998. Siemecks would be shuttered around the same time. Plenty of bars. 1919 down the comer. Lower Fells—the "foot of Broadway"—had Admiral's Cup and the Cat's Eye, my favorite. The place where the older rabble-rousers met. The guy with the peg leg. The old dancing Romeos—live music every night. Decorated in great dark nautical themes.

Across the street, *Homicide: Life on the Street* was filmed regularly. Yaphet Kotto, Andre Braugher, Richard Belzer—you could catch a glimpse of them as they filmed outside the Broadway Pier. My favorite show before I discovered *The Wire* a few years later. The Moran Company tugboats would come steaming into their berths next to the Broadway Pier every evening. Just watching them slowly glide into port made all seem right with the world. Broadway Market—one of the oldest in America—had an original UTZ potato chip stall, fresh meats, seafood, and a fantastic smell. Prevas's hot dog stand still sold a great hot dog (and even better gyros). Walking streets made of Belgian block where the tracks from the old B&O warehouse lines still were.

No trains had been pulled by those B&O switch tractors since 1984. American Can was a wasteland. Virtually all industry in the neighborhood aside from H&S Bakery had gone away. They can't outsource bread, right? A fast bike ride over to Ponca Street would bring you closer to the hum of an industrial city that had not yet died. They still made Chevys over at the plant on Holabird. GAF still made roof tiles. Far in the distance, you could see the plumes of smoke from Sparrows Point. Peterbilt and a soap factory. The port was always bustling. Trucks damaged S. Clinton Street so much I once nearly totaled my car just to get a look at the John R. Brown Liberty Ship back when we made things here, yes.

The path along the waterfront always brought peace. Anchorage had established the potential for this area as a prime waterfront development spot, but in 1996, it was still industrial. Captain James still served crabs on their outside deck. Sip and Bite was always a good place for a late-night snack. The Royal Farm at Fleet and Boston always seemed on the edge of something awful happening at any given time. The Go-Go Bar at Washington and Eastern kept their doors open late. The old, shuttered vegetable market still had an awning you needed to duck under. The duckpins at the Patterson. And of course, Kelly's, where Kelly and his wife served up beer, whiskey, crabs, soup, and karaoke with Kelly accompanying any Bob Dylan song on his very own harmonica just as good as the jester who stole the king's thorny crown.

It was a glorious time to be a twenty-two-year-old, first-year law student in a city that became my home.

I met community leaders. Wrote for the Upper Fells Point newsletter. Met Nick D'Adamo, John Cain, James Kraft—politicians. Voted for

Martin O'Malley after a *City Paper* editorial blasted Carl Stokes for his stance against gay people. Threw crab feasts in the street. Walked Citizens on Patrol with a big Newfoundland black dog named Bear—a prostitute once showed us her naked crotch on Eastern at 10:00 at night. We were not armed—probably should have been. Helped to get the President Street Civil War Museum opened with Captain Stevens Bunker, the legendary "pirate" who ran the South China Sea Marine Trading Company with a parrot on his shoulder and a pipe in his mouth. One of the people who stopped the road and saved the whole place.

Joined the Baltimore Streetcar Museum. Once rode a 1947 GM Baltimore Transit bus owned by a Catholic priest named Kevin from Fells Point to Middle River—endless waves and smiles on the avenue, especially from folks who remembered the #10 trackless trolleys. This same priest who owned this bus would later officiate my wedding. I shot pool against Danny Mills, aka "Crackers" from *Pink Flamingos*, at 1919 one week before I moved.

Was threatened by drug dealers. Once cleared snow by hand with all of our neighbors since the plows couldn't fit down the alley street. S. Chapel St. is an alley barely wide enough for one car. When the police would come to the house, occupied later by a dysfunctional family with a twelve-year-old, they would swarm from both ends of the block—like velociraptors from Jurassic Park. Once, she stole his dentures, and the two of them were rolling around in the backyard. I stuck my head over the cinder-block wall and hollered, "What the hell are you doing?" The husband screamed back, "She stole my teeth!" The wife used to steal tip money at Kislings Tavern. It wasn't funny, yet it was . . .

My clerkship in the circuit court started in September 1999. It was the centennial of Baltimore in 1997 and the centennial of the courthouse in 2000, "this noble pile" as H. L. Mencken called it. Largest monolithic columns in the world and the location for the filming of Al Pacino's *And Justice for All*. The Harbor Shuttle offered $30.00-a-month commuter service to the Inner Harbor. Best commute I ever had. The boat almost sank once when the tugboats were turning a sugar freighter and we came too close to the stern while under full power.

I would leave from the foot of Broadway and round out the day at Adrian's Book Café, where my best friend and roommate worked. His name was Morgan. He met his future wife there. We used to listen to Adam Sandler, throw *Pink Flamingos* parties, drink beer, watch *Braveheart*, and run the streets of Fells Point, screaming "Freedom" at the top of our lungs. It was like we were fourteen years old all over again.

We once heard a young mother walking by outside with her two children. We could not see them, only hear them. She yelled at her older son, "Donnie he shouldn't be doing that . . . hit him."

I moved in September 2001, one week before 9/11. After I left, a hot water pipe blew and flooded the whole house. When my uncle and I met to settle up the security deposit, the house was destroyed. He sold it to an investor who fixed it up.

There will never again be that wonderful era in the late 1990s when Upper Fells Point was still a true Baltimore neighborhood. Today, it is an inner-city bedroom community. I had a chance to experience it during its last gasp as a real neighborhood. For that I will always be grateful. Today, there is no wait at the Boston Street train crossing. Not like there used to be . . .

Yours until the Foot of Broadway wears a shoe,

The Magic Blanket

RON KIPLING WILLIAMS

My mother asked me one day in her Manhattan accent, "Why do you want to move to Baltimore? What's in Baltimore? They have nothing there. Why don't you move to New York? They have everything there."

I was stagnating artistically back in my home in Washington, DC. My dear friend Jim Vose (he and his wife, Stewart, have been running Area 405 for the better part of twenty years), who was moving to Baltimore himself, recommended that I make the transition. He said the city was inexpensive, friendly, and that I could figure things out while I was working on my craft.

So, my plan was to move to Baltimore and live there for a couple of years, get my stuff together, then move to New York, where I could really make my bones as an artist.

That was almost thirty years ago.

I have experienced what many have told me over the years. Baltimore is like a magnet. I do not know if there is some kind of cosmic vortex or some magical blanket that you never want to pull away, but there is something about this city that sucks you in and keeps you here. I have known a number of people who have moved away and come back.

One evening, I came up north to check out the place before my move. Jim took me to Louie's Bookstore and Café in Mount Vernon, on the upper crest of Midtown facing the Walters Art Museum. I stepped in from the yellowish streetlights and was instantly attracted to the popular two-story establishment. The first floor was the old-school, funky kind of bookstore, the smell of good books and wood.

Upstairs was the café, a cozy room where you could relax, remove your day, and have a delicious coffee drink. Their whole menu was delightful American fare. To this day I miss the potato skins. Their only drawback was that jerk of a waiter who thought he was too cool to work there, but somehow, he got stuck and *had* to serve us. One time there was a hair in one of my skins. I pointed it out to him. "Just pull it out," he said, head-tossing his golden-brown hair to the side.

Across the street was the Buttery, a diner like no other. This greasy spoon smelled like bug spray but served good, classic diner food, perfect for that after-hours meal. The waitress behind the counter looked like Broom

Hilda from the comic strip. You could count on some lively conversation as you devoured your bacon and eggs.

My first apartment was on 810 North Calvert Street, one block north from Center Stage, Baltimore's repertory theater. The rent was cheap, and the place was hot in the summer and cold in the winter, until the old radiator kicked in, and then it was blazing. I spent a good amount of time on a park bench between the Washington Monument and the architecturally gorgeous Mount Vernon Place United Methodist Church, journaling in my black-and-white composition notebook.

At night, there was a light and steady flow of prostitution up and down Calvert Street. I would listen to the transactional banter below as I rehearsed my spoken-word poetry, periodically staring up at my twelve-foot-high ceiling, walking in circles on my black Asian rug that covered the middle of the old burgundy painted living room wood floor.

My place was a couple of blocks away from the Hippo, the second-biggest gay establishment in the city behind Paradox (on Russell Street near Camden Yards) and the entertainment anchor of the gay community. Every second week in June, I just turned the corner, walked a hundred feet, and I was in the middle of Pride.

The Hippo reminded me of Tracks back in the day, the huge warehouse space turned gay nightclub south of Capitol Hill in DC. It was the most welcoming entertainment space in the city. Everybody and anybody was accepted. There was a big Plexiglas sign adhered to the front door, letting patrons know it was a gay establishment, that you must respect it or else you would either be prohibited from entering or escorted out of the building if there was any foolishness. The same rules applied at the Hippo, which, like Tracks, immersed their clubheads with drag balls, comedy nights, and jumping club music.

As a fan of independent films, I would walk a couple of blocks north of Penn Station and hit the Charles Theater, which at that time was a movie house of one, and every item had to be paid in cash. Afterward, I would cross the street and step into Club Charles, a warm and grungy bar, perfect for my post-punk sensibilities. Many of us transplants would end up there, ruminating about the day and hashing out politics, art, and philosophy over affordable adult beverages. We would do the same thing after dancing to old industrial and gothic music at the Depot right next door.

The Mount Royal Tavern was my first watering hole excursion when I landed in Charm City. Nestled between the buildings of the Maryland Institute College of Art on Mount Royal Avenue, it was an art-rocker-native haven. I had many belly laughs over drinks in this shotgunned and stripped-down spot, staring at the huge dark painting overhanging the wall behind the counter.

I am so glad I did not allow myself to get swallowed up and spat out in New York City. Of course, I would have returned to Baltimore licking my wounds, but why go through the pain, when I could do everything I needed to do here and shoot up to the Big Apple when necessary? In the years since my nonmove, I have traveled to other cities to perform, and whether it was Los Angeles, Philadelphia, or Miami, I never once thought, man, I have to move here. Baltimore was home for me.

Yes, we are a blue-collar town that lost big manufacturing and that consequently struggles with housing, education, and poverty. Yes, we have a high crime and drug activity rate, famously depicted in *Homicide: Life on the Street* and *The Wire*. Yes, we have major issues with race and policing, and we are still dealing with the aftermath of Freddie Gray.

But Baltimore has always been a city worth fighting for. You see it in the eyes of its people. There are generations of pride rooted in our neighborhoods. We live and breathe mutual aid, led by citizens ranging from neighborhood association members to community heroes like Bea Gaddy and Ruby Glover. We do not allow any outsiders to come in like great saviors and tell us how to run our city either. You either work with us, or you can get the hell out.

I would tell my mother now, Baltimore is where I got my sea legs, where I matured, where I met my wonderful family, where I made great friendships. It was where I got my first real introduction into the art scene, in a place called the BAUhaus (Baltimore Artist United House) next door to the Charles Theater, where I met its manager, and one of the most talented artists I know, Mark Sanders, formerly known as Bean.

Baltimore is the place where I went from being a poet on the open mic poetry scene to doing community theater at the Arena Players to becoming a solo theater artist; the place where I got my bachelor's and master's degrees and became an adjunct professor; and where I locked arms with movements like the United Workers, Baltimore Algebra Project, and Unite Here! for living wages, worker's rights, education funding, and an end to the school to prison pipeline.

Baltimore is that magical blanket for me, my feet resting on an old wooden floor, inside a sturdy row home.

Though I grew up in a big colonial-style home in the Rock Creek Park area of upper Northwest Washington, DC, I would not go back, nor would

I dare settle into the now highly developed and gentrified place I see when I visit. Gone are the old haunts in DuPont Circle, Columbia Heights, and the U Street corridor, replaced by million-dollar townhouses, high-priced bars and restaurants, and transplants who look at the natives as if they do not belong there.

Louie's Bookstore and Café, the Buttery, and the Hippo are no more—they were some of the charms of nineties Charm City—but my city has not done that extreme makeover. It is still the tough prizefighter, not letting anyone with an ill agenda come in the ring and take over.

Yes, there are high-priced development projects afoot, and yes, there are a few neighborhoods where they stick their noses up at you and act like you should not be there. But for the most part, when you become a Baltimorean, you are one of us.

Sitting in front of my laptop at the Bun Shop on Read Street, sipping my Vietnamese coffee and eating my Roti Boy pastry, I am thinking that it is funny how generations forget—like my mom, who was a beatnik back in New York's Greenwich Village in the fifties, who would have snapped her fingers listening to spoken word, or nodded her head during a lively political discussion at Red Emma's Coffeehouse and Bookstore.

The same woman who, as a student at San Francisco State University, walked through campus looking up at the National Guard pointing rifles down on the quad during the Vietnam era, would have been a MICA student hanging out at Mount Vernon Tavern, and she would have gone to art exhibits at the Maryland Art Place.

Though many choose to forget from where they came and the experiences they had, Baltimore has a way of keeping our history with us, with our old storytellers, the academic rabble-rousers from the sixties, dressed in corduroy jackets, slacks, and fishing hats, and flowered dresses and scarves, attending functions at St. John's Church or shopping at the Thirty-Second Street Market in Waverly, and schooling anyone in earshot.

I have listened to the stories from Grandmother Edna, Charlie Dugger, Mama Shirley, and other elders in West and South Baltimore who have loved, led, and taught children and families for generations. They were my real instructors on how to engage in effective community organizing and service.

I know now why I am here in Baltimore. In a way, I am Baltimore. I am a rough piece of marble step and a smooth column of marble art. I am not polished, but I shine anyway. I am scruffy, but I am fashionable. I have a lot of dents and dings, but my motor is always running. I am analog and I am digital. I am like a Maryland crab—sprinkle me with some O'Bay and

I taste good. And I am a long piece of fried lake trout at the Roost. I am a fine wine at Brewer's Art and a good cold Natty Boh. I am smart enough for good trouble, and good trouble enough to be smart.

No, Mom, allow me to disabuse you. I have everything I need right here in Baltimore, hon.

Triflin' Tulkoff

DEAN KRIMMEL

Original Tulkoff's location, East Lombard Street, Baltimore.
Credit: Tulkoff Family Archive.

"Don't touch the trifle until the Tulkoffs get here."

That's my mom talking, or at least how I remember it, the command directed at my older brothers as we gathered in the living room of our Belvieu Avenue semidetached in Northwest Baltimore.

Having our neighbors—Sol and Estelle Tulkoff of Baltimore's fabled horseradish family—over at Christmas had become a holiday ritual soon after we moved from Michigan to the Grove Park neighborhood.

The dining room table was filled with my mother's "sandies," cookies dusted with powdered sugar; "Christmas jewels," shortbread with a drop of jam in the middle; Rennie family shortbread from her father's side, and, from her stepmother, McCourt family fruit cake and nut bread.

In the center stood a glass bowl of trifle—maraschino cherries neatly arranged and dusted with finely chopped walnuts. Below this, a dark fruit cake surrounded by a wall of ladyfingers, all of it held together by two pints of homemade whipped cream.

A grand concoction worthy of display in the glass case at the Double T Diner on Rolling Road!

And I hated it. Not that anyone cared. My brothers and our father, Bob, loved those desserts. Yet, on Christmas Day in the Krimmel house, the only opinion that mattered belonged to Sol Tulkoff (1921–1988), son of the Minsk-born Harry Tulkoff, who founded the family horseradish business in Baltimore during the Great Depression.

Sol had fallen hard for Winnie Krimmel's trifle, probably around Christmas 1962, for the first time. As loud and self-confident as our family was midwestern reserved, Sol sang the trifle's praise while regaling us with stories of his latest sales trip to Las Vegas.

Hey, kid, let me show you my trick watch!

My mom beamed. Sol's seal of approval mattered.

Farewell to the Life of Kings

DOUG DONOVAN

I had just ended a call that began with me saying—maybe for the last time ever—"Hello, this is Doug Donovan, I'm a reporter for the *Baltimore Sun*."

Almost immediately, the voice of Samuel L. Jackson's character Jules from *Pulp Fiction* came to mind: "I been saying that shit for years. And if you heard it, that meant your ass."

I am certainly no Jules, much less Samuel L. Jackson. But a less lethal version of that same line applied nonetheless: I *had* been saying that shit for years (a dozen, to be exact), and for many public officials, it *did* mean their asses.

Just ask two disgraced Baltimore mayors, the nepotism-riddled city council of 2003, a defanged Maryland US attorney, a lying Baltimore County schools superintendent, and the state's self-interested regulators of the horse-racing industry.

I loved saying those words. And I got immense pride hearing my colleagues using the same refrain. I knew those words—"for the *Baltimore Sun*"—forever connected all of us to a legacy of kick-ass local, state, national, and international journalism dating to the paper's beginnings in 1837 all the way through the 2020 Pulitzer Prize the paper won for taking down a corrupt mayor and the conflict-riddled University of Maryland Medical System board.

Personally, the *Sun's* imprimatur emboldened me to forge through my own shy, people-pleasing traits to ask the next tough question and the next and the next. All those questions that blended in with that awkward, inconvenient cacophony of a constitutionally protected free press that no president, governor, mayor, hedge fund, or indifferent citizen will ever silence.

Not yet at least. Because they're forever trying. And for now, the hedge fund won. Alden Global Capital beat out the efforts of a Maryland philanthropist, Stewart Bainum, and others to establish local ownership of the *Baltimore Sun* and to treat it as a public trust, not as a cash-generating coupon shopper.

While the rich and powerful haven't been able to personally deliver a death blow to the general interest newspaper, the technological advances of the modern economy they helped build are carrying out the hit.

The end is near for the regional, general interest newspaper as the morons we so gently refer to as our fellow citizens (myself included) decide they'd rather navel gaze over the goings-on of their friends and extended social circles on FaceTikGram, to regurgitate predetermined views absent any debate with others who may differ with them.

You know, the things Americans have been doing since the beginning of a nation born and sustained by disagreements turned into compromises that have made us a better, more enlightened nation year after painful year.

The media has been a convenient foil for elected officials ever since a free press was established by the Founding Fathers, the old white dudes whom right-wingers are quick to invoke as saints for all they did to establish the God Bless United States of America, except for establishing that goddamned free press.

They call the media the fourth estate—after the legislative, executive, and judicial branches of our government. But it's in serious trouble. Especially on the local level.

I left the *Sun* in October 2019, afraid my chosen profession for nearly thirty years might not be able to sustain me to properly honor my duties to my three children.

I won't bore you with all of the social, cultural, and economic changes in our nation that led people away from mainstream media sources. To me those are think-tanky, Monday-morning-quarterbacking bullshit.

Truth is, the fat-cat executives in corporate media offices choked on the hair balls they accumulated licking each other's fluffy crotches. Seriously, it was just a few years ago—in 2017—that people were all aflutter that the *New York Times* had released a strategy for doing journalism in the digital age.

That's twenty years after Google started nibbling at the *Times'* lunch that the tech company now devours as a side dish.

I like to visualize the industry's best business minds as the Black Knight from *Monty Python and the Holy Grail*. They collectively refused to surrender to their enemies despite certain defeat as they stood on the one limb that hadn't been cut off.

"It's just a flesh wound!"

All the while, their enemies offered them chances. All refused. Radio had hacked away the first limb. TV took the second. The internet lopped off the third. And social media had been sawing through the trunk before a pandemic came along to finish the job.

Throughout the COVID-19 pandemic, my former *Baltimore Sun* colleagues were furloughed for weeks at a time, far better than being fired.

Still, Tribune Publishing was able to find $20,000 per quarter in 2020 as supplemental cash compensation for the added work to one of its executives who was making $234,000.

Newspaper staff are asked to do more with less (especially less money), but the executives get paid more when they take on a few added responsibilities. Must be nice. The corporate executives always find a way to keep increasing their pay on the backs of lower pay at the longtime local daily newspapers they're driving into obsolescence.

At least Tribune's board members took reduced fees for all the hard work they put in lifting those incredibly heavy rubber stamps.

I left in October 2019 after an amazing, exhausting reporting year, my twenty-fifth in the business. I saw no future for me in it, not without an early grave. Those who remain have to carry on the tradition the best way they can. At least until someone pries the *Sun* from the rapacious claws of Alden, the New York City hedge fund that will fatten its own returns by emaciating their product and the pay of those producing it.

Fewer people than ever can now say they are "from the *Baltimore Sun.*"

The only people to rejoice are corrupt leaders, like Trump and others in both parties, who never relent in selling the idea that the people dedicated to telling the truth are nothing but devious liars out to . . . to what? To get rich? Find me a rich reporter and I'll find you a lie-free utterance by Donald Trump.

People only see a reporter's final product. They never see the hours and days and weeks and months fighting for public information, demanding answers over and over, following up on inconsistencies. They don't see the courage it takes to challenge the most powerful among us while sitting alone in a room surrounded by that official's sycophants. Or having to make those imposing calls to grieving families for obituaries. Or showing up at murder scenes. Or exploring the substandard slums the poorest among us are forced to live in.

I could go on, but not anymore.

I'd been sitting on the front row of life since I was editor of my college newspaper. I did it for twelve years at the *Sun*. Working there provided me with the proudest moments of my professional life, and I'm sad I had to go.

After decades of afflicting the comfortable and comforting the afflicted, the *Sun* needs some love; it's work is too vital to lose.

I don't care if it's in print, on a phone or tablet, or being dictated by Alexa and Siri, the *Sun* must prevail no matter how much our ever-spinning world changes. Technology isolates us more and more each day. Elected officials divide us ever more deeply every passing minute of the 24/7, newsertainment day. But where do folks still turn to in a crisis? Newspapers.

The *Sun*'s motto—"Light for All"—has been around for 180 years, the positive precursor to the *Washington Post*'s more ominous "Democracy Dies in Darkness." That shift alone is telling. Fewer newspapers, less light. Less light, less democracy. Lessdemocracy, more darkness. More darkness, fewer newspapers.

Journalism is a serious business, even when the stories are humorous. That's because credible, accurate, and fair reporting—all the arduous steps reporters have to take before they write a word—is hard work. And it's made all the harder from all sides of the political spectrum: those in power, those who want to be in power, the Trump-humpers and the Bernie-bootlickers.

I despise certainty regardless of where I encounter it: Religious. Political. Sexual. Racial. Intellectual. Egomaniacal. That's one reason I love newspapers. There's always more than one side. Granted, one side may make far more sense, but that doesn't mean we censor the voices of the opposition.

It is worrisome that many newspapers are employing reporters who aren't afraid to wave their biases for all to see. You can't be a reporter with a slant because you will always carry with you a most deadly defect: "contempt prior to investigation."

You're no good to anyone if you're out there verifying what you already believe, seeing only what you choose. The best journalists deliver surprises, challenge conventional wisdom, and slay the sacred cows, even when it's one of their own doing the mooing.

Credit: Macon Street Books.

Growing Up in Baltimore as I Remember

WILLIAM DUPPINS

Where I come from, if you get to reach a ripe old age of fifty-three in Baltimore City, it's a milestone.

Reason being: Depending on where and how you grew up in Baltimore, being impacted by or confronted with tragic stories and situations can become so frequent that your psyche becomes numb.

The generation before me would tell stories of how tightly niched the family structure was, how one could sleep on their front porch all night or leave one's door unlocked without worrying. I now understand that Baltimore back then was a different time, but it's hard for me to imagine it that way in any era.

When I think about my parents growing up in Baltimore, it seems to be a simpler, more pleasant time. My childhood—and, as the years passed, ultimately my adulthood—had greater challenges. As I briefly relive these intervals of my life, some measure of pain will be revisited as well.

As far back as I can remember, childhood seems to be two sides of the same coin. My family, near the bottom of the lower income class, migrated from the south side of Baltimore toward the west side of the city. We settled into Northwest Baltimore near Pimlico racetrack in an area called Park Heights.

My family consisted of my grandmother, my mother, a great-uncle, three of my five uncles, and an aunt. I was only six months old—no siblings yet—when we moved into a house on Garrison Boulevard, two blocks from Park Heights Avenue.

Northwest was a step up for my family. It was 1968, and the Pimlico/Park Heights area was mostly a community of working-class and middle-class Jewish families. We were not quite a middle-class Black family, but we were moving in a positive direction. The money my three uncles had been able to send back to my grandmother from tours of duty in Vietnam made possible the move from South Baltimore to Northwest Baltimore.

My childhood there was full of adventure and fun. About the age of five, I remember attending preschool. The teachers spoke highly of me and often told my family how smart I was. When you're that age, it's common for adults to say positive things about a kid to the child's parents.

Honestly though, in my case, it was different, and my mother sought the counsel (I heard the whispering) of other family members when the school wanted me to start first grade early. It was decided that I should go at the normal pace.

But the attention, though positive, activated something inside of me. I believe this is where my personality split, and the decisions I would soon make were the cause of consequences and suffering.

In the presence of family, I conducted myself as they had come to see me. When alone or in the company of my choosing, I could act differently, and so I did. The way I acted outside of the family pleased me more, and these were the times that I was most content, even though the crowd I had gravitated to had no love or compassion for a kid celebrated for his intelligence.

With this crowd, popularity was a result of who you were, who you knew, or what you could do outside of the classroom. And so my athletic gifts were to my advantage. And so, as I became older, I was well liked by many in the neighborhood but more importantly by those who *mattered* in the neighborhood.

And in Park Heights, that can carry you a long way; it could even be a deciding factor between life and death.

I harbored dreams and aspirations of fame and fortune somewhere in the world of professional sports and took it seriously between the ages of nine and fourteen. I didn't apply the same energy in the classroom, and I continued seeking acceptance from the wrong crowd.

I also did not have a clue about how devastating the challenges would be that Baltimore presented. In the first year of junior high school—adolescence—my childhood ended. That's when drugs and crime, the things our city is not too fond of being recognized for, entered my life.

At first, because of my love of sports, I steered clear of marijuana. "No thanks," I'd say, "I'm an athlete." My commitment, however, didn't last long.

This was the early 1980s, an interesting time in Baltimore. I remember it like it was yesterday.

For me, it was a time of summer block parties, neighborhood camaraderie, and the prettiest girls around. And then, at least in Park Heights, the camaraderie collapsed when the longtime residents were forced to share the neighborhood with immigrants from Jamaica.

Like many neighborhoods in Baltimore, outsiders weren't welcome on our turf. Quarrels arose, accompanied by violence. But the Jamaicans had reefer, lots of it. So here came dollars and cents to defuse the tension. The merger of old and new was a no-brainer. Everybody made money, enough to sustain a partnership.

Through it all, I continued to dodge the positive values instilled in me by my family and continued to fall victim to the opposite way of life. I simply could not escape the allures of street life. I carried this well into adulthood, and it played out like a horror movie. If you're not on the lucrative end of the drug trade—and I was not—it can be painfully unsympathetic to your plight.

Once, when I was about twenty-two years old, I was watching *Monday Night Football* a few doors away from my grandmother's house with a friend. It was autumn. At halftime, I told my friend I had to go because my daughter's mother was busting my chops about not spending enough time with her. I left on my bicycle, which was on the front porch.

As I made my way to my daughter's mother's house, I noticed a guy standing on the corner. Something told me to keep going, but the thought of making a couple of extra dollars got the best of me. I stopped and asked the guy what he was looking for and began cruising next to him on my bike.

When he said he needed "about ten" of something, he grabbed me off the bike, threw me to the ground, and stuck a gun in my face.

With his other hand, he was digging in my pocket, yelling, "Kick it out! Kick it out!"

I kept telling him that I didn't have anything, making sure to roll on the side of the pocket he was trying to get into. By now, his accomplice, who I never saw standing in the alley, ran over and put *his* gun in my face. Now I was compliant. They took the money I had on me and moved down the alley.

As I got to my feet, gunfire rang out. As I fell to the ground, bullets seemed to whistle over my head. Across from the gunfight was a schoolyard, and I could see sparks from bullets ricocheting off the metal fence. I have never been so afraid of anything in my life.

This in contrast to my family, who went above and beyond to make sure I had a reasonable chance at succeeding in a challenging society. But a lot of it was self-inflicted, always going against what was instilled in me. I always yanked the dragon by the tail with no regard for consequences. Hindsight always comes at the end of the story.

Yet, there is still one last dream I have managed to salvage—to write my way out of my current situation into a positive one.

RECIPE:
Bradley Alston's Blues Bean Soup

Bradley Alston grew up in Baltimore's Madison Square neighborhood in the 1000 block of North Caroline Street on the east side. He attended a long shuttered Catholic grade school at the St Francis Xavier parish, graduating from the eighth grade in 1964. He is known as a longtime member, supporter, and officer of the Baltimore Blues Society, founded in 1986. For many years, he has written for the society's magazine—*Bluesrag*—and in those pages has written about everyone from Little Richard to Curtis Salgado.

Alston's "Blues Beans" have been a hit at many Baltimore Blues soirees, including the annual Alonzo's "Eat The Rich" Labor Day Weekend Picnics.

Prep: 45 minutes
Cook: 1½ hours (plus overnight)
Total: 2 hours
Yields: approximately 12 cups soup

Ingredients:
1 package of 16 Bean Soup, 16 oz. dry beans (can substitute medium dry lima bean)
2 smoked turkey legs (frozen)
1 large red pepper
1 large onion
1½ cup shredded carrots
1 cup chopped celery
1 tsp black ground pepper (two ½ tsp)
1 tsp garlic powder
1 tsp onion powder
½ tsp salt (adjust for your preference)
2 tsp margarine (optional)

The night before:

Add 2 smoked turkey legs to 12–14 cups of water in a slow cooker overnight (or 8 hours).

Soak 16 Beans Soup dry beans in water overnight, covered in refrigerator

The next morning (or 8 hours later):

Drain and rinse the soaked beans and place them into a large soup pot. Remove the smoked turkey legs from the slow cooker. Pour water/broth from slow cooker into soup pot. Separate turkey meat from the bones and discard the bones. Cut turkey meat into small size pieces and add to soup pot. Add to soup pot the chopped red pepper, onions, and celery; shredded carrot; and ½ tsp ground black pepper.

Heat on high for 15 minutes uncovered, stirring occasionally. Lower the temperature to a high simmer for 1 hour, covered.

Add to soup pot the garlic powder, onion powder, margarine, and the other ½ ground black pepper. Continue to cook on a low simmer, occasionally stirring, until beans are tender.

Joe and Mel vs. the Twist

DOUG LAMBDIN

After the Baltimore Colts won "the Greatest Game Ever Played" against the New York Giants in December 1958, they arrived back in Baltimore as world champions. Later that week, a house party celebration took place with players, wives, and girlfriends. To keep the charge of victory coursing through the party, Joe and Mel were hired again.

Joe was an unparalleled Dixieland-style banjo player, and Mel, a nearly deaf rhythm guitarist with an incredible "ear" and impeccable timing. They played standards from the 1930s and '40s and were the popular choice to entertain when the Colts gave parties.

Joe on banjo and Mel on the guitar. Mel is the author's father. Credit: Lambdin Family Archives.

Joe and Mel had tried different names for the act: the Stringbusters, the Dixie Duo. But in the end, they settled on how everyone knew them—Joe and Mel.

Relying on word of mouth, they rose through the ranks, bolstered at the time by a retro craze. They played private parties, local bars, college campuses, and local radio. Eventually, they headlined the Bayou in Washington DC and were once on a bill before 5,000 people at Baltimore's

Fifth Regiment Armory, where, in 1912, Woodrow Wilson was nominated to be the Democratic presidential candidate.

The following year, when the Colts beat the Giants in a repeat battle for the championship, Joe and Mel answered the world champions' call again. By day, Joe laid brick, a trade learned through the GI Bill. Mel sold pianos and organs. But it was their musical partnership they found most fulfilling, in spite of their laissez-faire approach to self-promotion. No doubt about it, Joe and Mel had reached a pinnacle.

As Baltimore's 1960 season got underway, the team needed to blow off some steam with a little off-field bonding. The remedy was a weekend party at "Big" Bill Pellington's with Joe and Mel providing the soundtrack.

When they arrived, Mel had his Epiphone guitar in one hand and Joe's Gibson Mastertone Banjo in the other, both in their cases as Joe didn't want anyone assuming he was a country musician. After the first strum, no one ever would. Mel wore a tie while Joe wore his collared shirt open to the chest.

The usual "Iron Horse" cast was in place: Gino Marchetti, Art Donovan, Lenny Moore, Raymond Berry, Johnny Unitas, "Big" Bill Pellington, Gene "Big Daddy" Lipscombe, Alan "The Horse" Ameche.

They were rowdy and loud, topping one another's dirty jokes and breaking into off-key songs. Bill Pellington was playing his usual party trick, completely covering someone's head with his giant hands, laughing, "Now you see 'em, now you don't." The beer was flowing and glasses were being raised in cheers by the time Joe and Mel had set up.

In a fit of showmanship, Joe and Mel would mill about a corner of the room, seemingly still adjusting and tuning their instruments, when Joe would nod to Mel and they would turn in unison and pound the opening chords to their first song, an up-tempo, rousing version of "Whispering."

Their motto was from the first note: *Hit 'em right between the eyes.* The Colts and their wives and girlfriends would spin around and begin cheering the raucous Dixie style.

Like a runaway train, Joe and Mel were rollicking through their first set, the union-requisite forty minutes on and twenty minutes off. They had just finished the final chorus of "Five Foot Two" and announced their break. It was then that a hand shot up at the back of the room, and a voice exclaimed, "I got iiiit!"

All heads swiveled at once. In a raised hand, like a brandished chalice, was a 45 rpm record. On the record player it went, and in a moment, a snare drum hit a fast four-four beat, before the singer invited his girl to grab his hand and dance.

And thus, they could twist all night.

It was Chubby Checker, and the song was "The Twist," a summer hit that shot to number one on the top forty in the first month of the 1960 NFL season. And the gyrating began. Joe and Mel's entire twenty-minute break turned into an endless loop of the two-minute-and-thirty-four-second song.

Twistin' time, most certainly, was here.

As Joe and Mel began their next set with "Bill Bailey," which had always been a crowd favorite, the partygoers dispersed back into conversation. From the stage, a few dramatic sighs could be seen. Joe and Mel were losing the crowd. These were uncharted waters. Joe leaned into Mel's good ear and bellowed one word—*saints*.

Fifteen years of timing and shorthand built into a musical relationship, Mel knew precisely what Joe was aiming for: *Let's pull out the big guns.*

"When the Saints Go Marchin' In" was always the showstopper, their encore, the one that had them stomping the floorboards. Mel's unshakable timing and Joe's slick, effortless slides and lightning runs could create frenzy.

On New Year's Eve, they would create such a furor with "Saints" that they would lead the crowd out the front door, down the block, and into strangers' homes, pied pipers parading around families sitting before their televisions, waiting for Guy Lombardo to count down to the new year.

They launched into "Saints," their arms like pistons pounding out the chords. The crowd offered a faint elevated interest, some nods, a few tapping feet. Joe and Mel finished their set, and by the time they reached the deli trays from Nate's and Leon's, Chubby Checker was already into the second verse.

Usually, Joe and Mel would enforce a self-imposed professional rule and wait until the second to the last break to imbibe. But now, they each took a beer glass from the tray and filled it to the top from a pitcher of Gunther's. They leaned against the wall, invisible, not being able to look away from the tableau before their very eyes—the party trying to keep up with Chubby.

Each dancer was "twisting" in place, one foot planted and pivoting while the other was raised beneath, like drunken flamingos with crew cuts and bouffants. Each under the same magic spell. Joe and Mel turned away to pile plates full of cold cuts and feasted, as they watched the sons of Baltimore and their significant others twist the night away.

Unlike years past, when Joe and Mel would leave with autographed footballs and echoes of "Encore!" trailing them, this night, they packed up early with only their pay, a handshake, and an unfulfilled promise of "See you next time" to see them off.

Joe had his banjo in hand, and Mel had his guitar as they closed the door behind them and walked down the drive to Joe's car. No words spoken, just Chubby Checker's voice calling after them.

The Colts went six and six that year after winning back-to-back championships. And Joe and Mel never played another Colts party.

Fran's Bar: A Short Story

JEN GROW

The bar door opens halfway and two people poke their heads inside. "Fran," they say, "Your mother is doing it again." A sliver of sunlight shines into the bar. It's late afternoon.

A woman with frizzy hair looks up. She slides off her seat behind the counter and walks around the bar. She's slow about untying her apron. "Linette," she says to a woman with a skinny ponytail, "you're in charge of things. Keep track of who buys what."

Linette nods. Her body is as thin as her ponytail.

The woman with the frizzy hair—Fran—walks toward the door as though she's unsure she wants to leave. "And no free rounds this time," she says over her shoulder. Then she grabs the hand of one of the people at the door and walks outside.

The bar is quiet for a moment. The place is mostly empty except for a few people who sit on the stools motionless, their elbows on the bar. There's an old cigarette machine in the corner, mirrored beer signs on the wall. A yellowed painting of France rattles in its frame as a bus roars by outside. In the back of the bar, a shuffle bowl table squawks in an automated voice every ten minutes or so. "Step up and take a chance! Give it your best shot!" it calls out. Then it cackles.

No one looks up. There's the rustle of newspaper pages, and then a spring squeaks on the ladies' room door. A woman in a tank top and jeans comes out. Her tank top barely covers the roll of her stomach. She tugs on her tank top, trying to pull it down as she walks across the scuffed tile to her stool.

"Where's Fran?" she leans over and whispers to an old woman at the end of the bar.

"Her mother," the old woman says.

"Oh."

The old woman swirls a bent finger on the bar, drawing invisible pictures next to her beer glass.

"I don't know if she's crazy or if she's blessed," someone further down the bar says, a heavy-set woman with faded tattoos.

"Who?" the tank top woman asks.

"Fran's mother."

"She's lovesick," Linette says. "That's what she is." Linette takes the rubber band out of her hair and loosens her ponytail. She combs the knots out of her hair with her fingers, then gathers her hair back into a ponytail again.

"You'd think they would've come up with something for that by now," the woman in the tank top muses. She's got her thumb in her mouth, chewing at the nail.

"Oh, Mary Alice, they've got pills, all right. Fran's mother is hooked. That's why she has these fits."

"No," the tank top woman, Mary Alice, says, "I mean, they should come up with a pill for love that makes it easier in the long run. Less of a pain in the ass."

"Yeah. Right, Mary Alice. The pill you're looking for is sitting right in front of you. It's in liquid form." Linette takes a gulp from her own glass, empties it, sets it back on a cocktail napkin.

Mary Alice bites at her fingernail, tears at it with her teeth. She spits a piece into the ashtray next to her. "I've never seen Fran's mother in the middle of a fit," she says. "Just heard about it, like it's epilepsy or something."

"It's not epilepsy," Linette says. She reaches across the bar to pour herself another draft. She makes a mark on the napkin in front of her. "Epilepsy don't explain the howling and all the time chasing men down the street. Fran's mother looks like a beat-up Betty Boop. What with her bangs and dyed black hair, her crooked skirts and ripped up pantyhose. She thinks she's a beauty, which is the sad part."

"Now I know who you mean. I didn't know *that* was Fran's mother," Mary Alice says.

"So you know what I'm talking about," Linette says. "It's definitely not epilepsy." Linette inspects the split ends of her ponytail.

"I gotta hand it to her, she won't give up," says the woman with faded tattoos. Her arms are wide and thick, the tattoos stretched and shapeless. "Whatever it is, Fran knows how to handle it." She lights a cigarette and keeps talking with it pursed between her lips. "She's been doing it since she was a kid. Last time, she pulled her mother in here, kicking and screaming, and let her play on the shuffle bowl table for free."

"It gets expensive going to the hospital every time."

"Oh, I know it," the women say back and forth to each other.

Afternoon sun filters through a small window at the end of the bar. None of the bar lights are turned on yet. There are shadows, a fan overhead, cigarette smoke scrolling toward the fan. On the bar, beer bottles and juice glasses are half-filled with draft beer; nickels, dimes, a few quarters; the coins are wet from small beer puddles.

The old woman with bent fingers reaches into the pocket of her housecoat to count out her change. She pushes her pennies to the side as she counts. She taps the bar in front of her juice glass and slides sixty cents across to Linette who reaches in the cooler and hands her an Old German beer bottle. Linette takes a pen and makes another mark on her napkin.

"I wonder what's going on. Should we see what's going on?" Mary Alice asks.

Somebody coughs.

"Fran can handle it," another woman says, a new voice in the conversation. "These fits are routine. Everyday hysteria." The woman who says it has got the newspaper open in front of her. Only part of her face is showing, her wide unplucked eyebrows.

Mary Alice gets up from the barstool and walks over to the jukebox. She flips the pages, looking for the right number.

"Don't play that song again," Linette says. "I've got a splitting headache."

"I'm just looking," Mary Alice answers.

"You keep singing the wrong words, anyway."

"I do not."

But soon, Mary Alice is back on her wobbly barstool, moping and picking at a bug bite on her leg.

There's the sound of a siren outside. The pitch rises and falls as it passes. Then the rustle of newspaper as the woman reading it fights the pages to fold them up, again. She goes, "I used to have this guy serenade me all the time. He was a fat guy. It was pretty sad, too. He used to sit in his car, singing with the radio, even in winter."

"I remember that guy; his name was Frank."

"Yeah, Frank. Remember him?" The tattoo woman takes a long drag from her cigarette, and smoke rolls from her mouth as she speaks. "Mavis, what was the name of his friend who pretended not to know him when other people were around?"

"Old John," Mavis says. She finishes folding her paper and puts it aside. "The two of them would sit in the car and listen to the Orioles game."

"I remember that guy," someone says again.

"And Frank," Mavis shakes her head, "always singing that same song." She looks into the bottom of her juice glass, then slides it toward Linette. "As soon as he'd see me walking down the street, he'd get out of his car and start performing. Take his cigar out of his mouth, spread his arms wide, and start singing."

"What'd you do?"

Linette pulls another Old German out of the cooler and slides it toward Mavis.

"I told him no thanks. I told him, 'Frank, get back in your car.'"

A barstool scrapes against the linoleum in the middle of Mavis's story. The old woman with the bent fingers gets up. She shuffles across the floor to the bathroom. The spring on the door squeaks when she opens it.

"I said it a thousand times, 'Frank, go home,' like I was talking to a dog. But this one time, he wouldn't stop singing, even after I went inside. He was out there on the street, yelling. Well, I closed the windows. He was just trying to get attention. That's how he was."

"I know it," the women say.

"This one time," Mavis says, her cheeks red with spider veins, like she's winded from telling her story, "I just ignored him and went inside to take a shower. When I came out, I seen all these lights flashing on the street. The police, the amb'lance. 'What the hell?' I think. I look outside and there's Frank strapped on the gurney. They put him in and drove away."

Water runs through the pipes when the toilet flushes. Then the spring on the door squeaks, and the old woman comes out of the ladies' room.

"What happened to Frank?" Mary Alice asks.

"I don't know," Mavis answers. "I open the window and I yell, 'Hey John!' And he goes, 'What?' and I go, 'What's with Frank?' And he just shrugs and pretends like he don't know because there are all these other people around."

"I'll be damned," the old woman rasps. She doesn't seem to be listening to their story but is rooting through her pockets and pulling out pennies.

Linette doesn't say anything. She picks up the old woman's glass and pours her a beer from the tap.

"So you never found out what happened?" Mary Alice asks.

"No. I never did," Mavis says. "Later I heard he was rolling on the sidewalk in his underwear. But I missed it; I took a shower and missed the whole thing."

"I do that. I miss everything," the women say to each other.

"Oh, me too."

It's quiet for a moment. The fan blows. Dust balls stir on the floor with the breeze. Then the shuffle bowl table starts talking. "Step up and take a chance!" it cackles, like a reminder for the women to stretch and move, to do something different.

Mary Alice tugs her tank top down. Somebody flicks a lighter. A minute later, a hacking cough, a phlegmy sound. Linette is the one who's coughing, bent over with her hand in front of her mouth. It's as if she is trying to expel something. The other women are quiet.

When she gets a breath, she says, "My mother tells me all the time, 'Linette, what's wrong with you. You used to be beautiful.'"

"I miss everything," Mary Alice says again.

Mavis refolds the paper. "Listen to this in the *Shopper's Guide*," Mavis says. "Vasily Sarvenko was charged with first-degree murder in the stabbing death of Serov Stevenson. Stevenson, who lived upstairs from the Ann Street Laundromat, was discovered dead in his apartment by neighbors who were doing laundry at the time."

"I remember hearing about that," the woman with the stretched tattoos says. "I heard some woman saw blood dripping from the ceiling. She screamed so much she hyperventilated and fell over. The paramedics had to treat her before they could take the body away."

"I was going to do my laundry that day. But I didn't. I can't remember why not," Mary Alice says.

"All I know is, you couldn't get a washing machine for a week. The place was packed, everybody pretending to do laundry while they snooped around," the tattoo woman says.

"Oh, I know."

"Police believe Stevenson's death is the result of a long-standing feud between Gypsy families," Mavis reads.

No one answers for a minute or so. Even the shuffle bowl table is quiet.

"I've got to get out of the city. How can people live like this?"

Mary Alice is the one who says it. "I want to go somewhere beautiful and serene like in that picture."

"That picture?" Linette says as she pulls two beer cans out of the cooler—one for her, one for Mavis. "Mary Alice, you dream about love too much."

"That picture's not there to be beautiful. It's there to cover up a hole," the tattoo woman says.

The women laugh.

"I remember that," Mavis smiles and shakes her head. The spider veins on her cheeks make her look flushed. "Fran's mother thought she was a majorette that day and came in the bar twirling a stick. She wanted to prove how high she could kick and put her foot through the paneling."

"You got to admit, she could kick pretty high," Linette laughs.

"That's true. But then she cried and couldn't stop. It was like she was grieving her whole life."

The women are quiet.

"I still want to go," Mary Alice answers. "Go to France and walk on that street."

"Step up and take a chance!" the shuffle bowl table cackles.

The old woman taps her nickels on the bar with her bent fingers. "Hey," she says, as if she's trying to get Linette's attention. But she turns her stool toward Mary Alice and says, "I almost went there after the war. I was in love with a GI and had my bags packed."

"What happened?" Mary Alice says.

Linnette and Mavis and the tattooed women exchange quick glances.

"Honey. That time's past. You're sitting right here next to me, so it was not meant to be," the old woman says. "You're already gone. Stop daydreaming. That picture is as close as any of us will get."

The women turn in their seats to look at the painting. All but the old woman who's hunched on her barstool, sipping her beer.

The blues and greens and grays in the painting are washed out. Small dark figures—gentlemen in top hats, ladies in gowns—stroll arm in arm in the drizzle, holding umbrellas, the Arc de Triomphe gray and hazy in the background.

The bar is dim. The sun has shifted outside, late afternoon to evening. No one moves to turn on the overhead lights. Outside, sirens wail in the background like far-off birds calling to each other.

Our Lady of Pigtown: A Short Story

RAFAEL ALVAREZ

On May Day 2020—just before the United States splintered into dozens of warring confederacies—eight-year-old Amber Willis passed the usual band of sick, deranged, and desperate people that lived on the streets she took home from school.

Varied in all things but circumstance—is there a population more diverse than the poor?—each lived a few tenuous clicks below the challenges Amber had faced all her life. Many of them had gotten off to better starts than the girl with the curly red hair, a stubborn orphan who lived alone on the edge of downtown in a godforsaken neighborhood called Pigtown.

But none of them had her heart. Or the freckles that covered her face; a terrible constellation that crossed the bridge of her nose, left to right, up and down. Amber was not someone who could easily hide.

Among the residents of the curbs and median strips were drug addicts, a grandmother long removed from family and medication, and a gaggle of cursed sons-of-bitches who swore they would die for one another but had not yet gotten the chance. It was a slow day of panhandling when Amber walked by, and it struck her that none of them, who begged something of her every day, asked for money. A cigarette. Or a cold drink of water.

Today, with just a few weeks left in the school year, each addressed her with different twists on the same theme.

One, nodding spastically, chattered: "Good, good, good, good, good . . ."

The next guy—supine with flies, black and green, buzzing around the soiled crotch of his pants and his scabbed, runny nose—said to her every day, his voice dripping with all the erections he'd never have again, "You fine."

But today he merely whispered: "You're good . . ."

Splayed out in a broken beach chair, a woman incessantly stroked her arms beneath a filthy blanket, turned out of a public psych ward the day before, naked beneath a flimsy gown and paper slippers. She cooed: "You *are* good."

This last spoke to Amber just before the girl turned off of West Pratt Street and into the alley where she lived. And in a voice as sane as yours or mine, said: "Believe it . . ."

Amber passed without haste or tarry, walking with the quiet determination she put into the to-and-fro each day, striding toward home to lock the door against a what-are-you-looking-at town of fervent improbability, a place ribboned with cruel stretches of asphalt where making it from breakfast on Tuesday to dinner on Wednesday put you ahead of the game.

Baltimore—a port city as old as any in the United States, older than the nation, the cradle of American Catholicism where providence amounted to what had been revealed the day before, only darker.

Home was a few blocks past the B&O Roundhouse, and once there, Amber plopped down at the kitchen table and made herself a snack with what was left of that week's peanut butter and crackers, ran some tap water in a plastic cup illustrated with an orange cartoon bird, and settled in to do her homework.

The adults who called the squat-and-narrow house on Woodyear Street home came and went, fended for themselves, and dosie-doed from one swinging partner to the next; usually whomever had what they needed to get through the next five minutes. None were blood kin to Amber.

No one was home when she took out her notebook and some colored pencils. No one had been home yesterday or the day before and very soon, neither would she.

In school—Edgar Allan Poe Elementary—Amber's class was reading fables, folktales, and myths. In math, they were learning about money—how to earn it and how it is spent, both wisely and otherwise.

(In less than a week, there would be no school, neither in the suburbs nor the city as terror and sedition erased dotted lines that people once believed would keep them safe.)

Most of the other kids in Amber's class were obsessed with money, parroting what they heard at home and on the street, bragging about what they were going to do when they were rich. Amber wondered if money allowed someone to be left alone to do what they wanted.

She took a library book from her backpack (the public library, her school did not have one) and opened it to an opulent illustration of a rooster and a hen. Then, on a blank page of her composition book, in block letters across the top, she wrote with a thick marker: DIRTY TRICKS.

Below that, in a fluid, elegant cursive of which she was most proud, Amber copied out the story in the book, changing the words as it suited her, savoring the freedom of it.

Mr. Rooster and his wife Jenny Hen made a carriage out of a large oyster shell with bottle caps for wheels. Rooster strapped himself to the carriage with wet spaghetti and pulled his wife down to the harbor to find crabs for supper.

Amber lived—it would be a stretch to call it a home—a few blocks beyond the B&O Roundhouse . . . Credit: Jerome Gray.

"Let's go to the water before the rats eat them all," said Rooster.

And Jenny answered, "Just let 'em try . . ."

Reaching into her bag for crayons to draw the oyster chariot, Amber was jerked from her reverie when a rubber ball smacked the window above the sink. There, she saw her two best friends, pretty much her only friends—Douglass and Butchie. They were a few years younger than her; two little fuck-ups who listened to every word she said but heeded none of it. Butchie and Douglass, as loyal as dogs.

The boys were all but illiterate, knowing how to write their names and read simple signs like STOP while pronouncing words the way everyone they knew did—in a thick, largely unintelligible Baltimorese.

Butchie had the ball back in his hands, rearing back to hurl it again.

"AMBER, COME OUT AND PLAY!"

Throwing the window open to tell the knuckleheads to cut it out, Amber's words caught in her throat when she saw words written in the clouds above the tarred rooftops:

"I never played with dolls like other girls. I never played at all. They had me working before I went to school . . ."

Several of the clouds stopped drifting and began to change color—becoming darker, slowly, like the bark of a young tree—arranging themselves into the shape of . . .

"What, Amber?" said Butchie in the same annoyed voice everyone used with him, watching as the bewildered girl came out of the house. "I didn't break anything."

Amber walked past the boys without speaking. They followed, standing close behind as she stared into the sky, up to the very top of a giant ailanthus that long before had pierced the roof of an abandoned house in the middle of Kuper Alley.

Amber stopped at the edge of the yard, a pen of weeds, rat burrows, and trash overtaking a house no one had lived in since crack swept through in the 1980s, a forgotten scourge that took the lives of Amber's parents. She opened her mouth but, once again, could not speak.

The vision, now a shimmering light of bronze in the shape of a woman, did.

"You're good . . ."

With all his might, Butchie threw the ball at the spot of Amber's gaze and missed by a mile, giggling as it fell through the collapsed roof. The children faced the back of the house, long torn away to reveal rooms where generations had eaten, slept, fought, prayed, cursed, listened to the radio, and made love; nine layers of wallpaper and a hundred years exposed to the elements like a dollhouse at a yard sale.

Deep inside the building, the ball was lost forever.

"That was mine," said Douglass.

"Then go get it," said Butchie.

No one moved.

Eyes skyward, Amber edged closer to the yard. In the uppermost branches of the tree floated the luminous apparition, shimmering in a thousand shades of brown. The specter wore a translucent gown as blue as the Maldives, her bare shoulders reflecting the sun as the orb began its late afternoon descent.

The mammoth tree of heaven—a genus once used for medicine, leaves like green spears—had begun as an ignored weed when the house was the home of railroad laborers.

Ghetto palm, roof buster, brick eater.

Pedestal.

The boys saw nothing.

"Amber," said Douglass.

"Amber," called Butchie.

Nothing but the bulk and reach of the tree and ankle-deep trash around it.

Amber drew closer to the house; neck bent back, eyes up in wonder. Anxious that she might fall into the exposed basement—a pit of broken bottles, rusty syringes, and feces animal and human—Butchie reached for Amber, but Douglass held him back.

"You're good," the Brown Lady said again as Amber trembled. "Good enough to listen . . . nobody listens."

And bestowed upon the eight-year-old a secret and an assignment. Out of love for Douglass and Butchie—standing dumbfounded behind her, unable to fathom anything not shouted in their faces—Amber asked if there was a message for them.

There wasn't.

The multiverse, as Amber soon learned, only selects filaments strong enough to carry its current, if just for a moment. She had been chosen as the first to know what was about to convulse the United States, a seed as flowering and stubborn as the mighty ailanthus of Kuper Alley.

This first secret put a shovel in the girl's uncalloused hands. And promised that she would never go hungry again, no matter how bad life became. Two more would follow.

"AMBER!" Butchie yelled, "WHAT?"

Amber nodded to the sky—*"understood"*—turned her back on the boys and went inside.

"Please Amber," pleaded Douglass, who never asked anyone for anything. "What happened?"

By age six, Butchie's shoulders had become permanently hunched because he walked with his head down, looking for pennies and dimes that people who didn't have two nickels to rub together believed themselves too good to keep. His dreams were bathed with rivers of turkey sandwiches, mashed potatoes, and chocolate milk.

Douglass lost his little sister when a car ran a stop sign and ever since had hoarded baby dolls, adding to the girl's collection. He rescued them from gutters and trash cans (once from the back of a moving garbage truck) from one end of Pratt Street to the other; Pigtown to Patterson Park. For this, he was often beaten up.

After a few minutes of silence, the boys wandered off and went their separate ways. Amber lay across her bed and wondered why she—who'd never known what she believed—had been burdened so.

The kid lived in the midst of a murder a week, multiples on weekends, and once, a dozen shot dead between Christmas and the New Year. And life rolled on. Now, the gods were about to turn the shores of the Patapsco into rubble.

Mister Rooster pulled Jenny Hen down to the docks along Pratt Street where they found a pier scattered with crab shells not yet picked clean and a half-dozen newly dead crabs, too small for the pot.

Once they had eaten their fill, on a shortcut home to Pigtown, they found the way blocked by Ronnie the Rat.

"The Civilities" were neighbor-upon-neighbor, kin-against-kin, US vs. THEM terrorism that broke the United States into a continent of noncontiguous confederacies.

Long simmering (some 160 years of hatred and resentment, fresh hostility added with each wave of immigration), the wars exploded with the unprecedented refusal to transfer power, as though George Washington had chosen a throne instead of going home to tend to his crops.

And yet, the battle provided Amber with a family that cared and a better quality of life than she'd ever known, a shovel in her hands at the age of nine, a gun by thirteen; hard, filthy work, honest and necessary.

The second time the Brown Lady appeared to her, Amber was digging a trench—2.5 feet by 8 feet—in a long-abandoned graveyard behind a used tire store in West Baltimore. She was paired in the St. Peter the Apostle cemetery with Chain Smoking Joe, an elderly Vietnam vet who'd come out of hibernation to serve the cause.

They were burying a partisan who'd been killed in a raid to take back a library that no one had used in a decade. The corpse truck arrived twice a day.

Leaning on her shovel and looking up to shield her eyes as the old soldier kept digging (pick and axe, spade and shovel; a backhoe attracting too much attention), Amber saw the gathering wisps of the Brown Lady bearing a smile that wasn't quite a smile, though it could not be mistaken for anything else.

Joe looked but saw nothing more than Douglass and Butchie had: an eerily silent girl staring into the clouds in a posture of submission. Though Amber more than held her own in their labors, Joe didn't ask much of her. The Lady was not so lenient.

"Why him?" asked Amber as the Lady dispersed across the horizon. "He never hurt anyone."

As the last pixels of the specter dissolved, the truck arrived with four new bodies and lunch. Joe leaned against a tombstone (Philip Berrigan, 1923–2002), and Amber sat cross-legged on the ground facing him, eating sandwiches and drinking water from the hose that ran up to the old rectory.

Joe lit the butt of a cigarette: "Who were you talking to?"

Amber: "No one."

"Who was talking to you?"

Amber, able to lie and tell the truth at the same time, one of the skills that made her valuable, said, "Doesn't every kid have an imaginary friend?"

Joe: "I had an imaginary friend in Vietnam."

Amber: "What happened?"

Joe: "I came home, and he didn't."

———————

Ronnie hissed as a dozen compadres behind him squealed and bared their teeth.

"Thieves!" Freeloaders! Who invited you?"

But the Rooster was from Pigtown, and it was easy to tell that the Rat, whispered Jenny Hen, "ain't from around here."

When Rat leapt for Rooster's throat, Jenny flipped the oyster shell into a shield, and the cock—the blood of the islands in his veins—turned savage, hacking the rodent with his beak and claws.

And the vermin that just a moment before had bragged that they had Ronnie's back, scattered.

———————

Word, of course, got out. And no one, not even the beggars along the route that Amber walked when school still existed, believed the children. The boys did because Amber did. Butchie defended Amber to the point of violence, and Amber eventually forgave herself for spilling the beans, telling herself what the Lady never did: It would not have changed a thing if she'd kept her mouth shut.

She was thirteen and the boys eleven when Douglass was murdered while rummaging through a trash can near the Roundhouse, it's circular roof collapsed for the second time in its long history. The first by a wet, heavy show. The second by a bomb dropped from a drone a day after it had been commandeered for a field hospital.

Douglass's murder had nothing to do with the Civilities. In Crabtown, senseless violence remained undefeated. The boy thought he'd seen the thin plastic arm of a decapitated doll sticking through the wire mesh of the can, on the side of which was a sign that said: TRASH BALL / A NEAT GAME / A NEAT CITY.

The Lady appeared to Amber for the last time at the funeral mass at St. Peter Claver, Pennsylvania and Fremont, not far from the tire store cemetery. The corpse truck was making a run to that side of town, and Amber hopped a ride. Outside the church stood a ring of guards, all volunteers, all armed; half of whom did not trust the other half.

Douglass's casket was front and center, just before the altar where a priest from Cameroon—who had come to Baltimore as a missionary and now couldn't get out—celebrated the Eucharist.

Amber sat in a pew by herself, not more than a dozen people in attendance, including the priest and a seventy-five-year-old altar boy. Butchie, in the very back pew, had stayed up all night trying to figure a way to sneak a tiny doll into Douglass's casket. He'd never been in a church of any kind before.

And thus, he was not curious as to why the faces of the statues—all of them, Jesus, his Mother, her husband Joseph, and a dozen others lining the walls—had been painted black.

(Paint it black, you devils.)

A bunch of Black Power Catholic kids had done a middle-of-the-night makeover in 1967, inspired by Stokey and Huey and Angela but launched the week the Chambers Brothers released "Time Has Come Today."

The revolution was just around the corner: *"Can't put it off another day . . ."*

They had no idea.

Barely teenagers at the time, maligned by a mature congregation who still thought of themselves as "colored," the troublemakers were now respected elders, the ringleader on the altar assisting the priest with Communion.

It is doubtful that Ossawa Tanner himself could have accurately portrayed Amber's Lady—now brown, now bronze, now chestnut—as she hovered in the choir loft above Douglass's casket.

Cinnamon, sensed but not seen as she sang her heart out with a half-dozen women in white robes who knew that they'd never sounded so good. When the mourners sang, "Come for to carry me home," Amber heard, "Choose my will where your nose meets the unselected future of your life . . ."

Throughout the service, no request was made of Amber, and she wondered, perhaps, if this was just hello. Of course, it was more than that, more before goodbye. The last message was an order, a tall one.

"Make for me a little flower upon the spot of the great ailanthus, build it as high as a pigeon without disturbing the tree . . ."

Downstairs, at a small reception in the church hall, Butchie washed down two jelly doughnuts with lemonade and stuffed his pockets with cheese sandwiches.

Amber watched him from across the room and smiled (some things never change) as she took a chair next to Douglass's grandmother. When she did, the church ladies comforting the grieving woman excused themselves, and Butchie waved to Amber before scooting upstairs. They would never see each other again.

In the vestibule, Butchie dropped the doll he'd hoped would accompany his friend to the other world in a collection basket and pushed his way into the bright sun of the day. With the sandwiches melting in his pockets, he began walking south for no other reason than it seemed better than any other way.

Amber nibbled a pretzel, and Douglass's grandmother, who'd prayed every night of the dead boy's life that Baltimore would not take him as it had thousands of others, sipped ginger ale and rubbed the veins on her hands.

"It's ready whenever you are."

"Thank you, young lady."

"Just you and the priest, ma'am. Not safe for anyone else."

"Of course," said the grandmother. "I understand."

Mister Rat now bleeding, now begging, now dead.

Back at the cemetery, waiting for Douglass's body, Amber found Joe at work, slow and steady, shovelful by shovelful.

"How'd it go?"

"You know," said Amber.

"Yeah," said Joe, "I know."

"I heard you used to be a bricklayer."

"That too. What are we building, kid, a bunker?"

"Something like that," said Amber. "After we take care of my friend, I'll show you where I grew up."

As longtime Baltimore reporter Tom Nugent often called locals, "The doll dead of Crabtown . . ." Credit: Jennifer Bishop.

What I Miss about Baltimore

REESE CASSARD

I left Baltimore on a Friday. For roughly the past 182 Fridays, that meant happy hour. But on this Friday, it meant packing my Subaru and embarking on the first leg of a three-day, 1,600-mile trek to Boulder, Colorado, with a couple duffle bags of clothes and my girlfriend's six-month-old border collie, Bauer.

I was excited to reunite with Kate. I was anxious to start my new life. I was angry Subaru refused to pay me for literally living one of their commercials. I was nervous Bauer might vomit. But mostly I was sad to miss happy hour in Baltimore.

Happy hour, a tradition celebrated around the world, is different in Baltimore. Just before moving out of my parents' house outside DC, a neighbor who grew up in Baltimore joked that I would find a bar and a church at every corner, and that most of them were in the same building. It took me a year to realize he was serious. I ended up living in Baltimore for nearly four years—one in Federal Hill, a summer in Timonium, and the rest in Canton—and every time I was in a bar, I could see a church from the window, and I could have hit another bar with a baseball.

For all the nicknames Charm City has accumulated over time, I can't believe none of them address this. I propose "Where God Drinks."

I drank a lot in Baltimore. It's shameful to think that's what comes to mind first when reflecting on that chapter of my life, but it's the truth. Finally, out of my parents' house, I was making real money for the first time, and everywhere I turned were friends eager to carouse. I know.

I miss it all terribly. The crisp Natty Boh beer during brick-insulated winters. The sugar-filled Orange Crushes during asphalt-miraged summers. The rooftop decks and the drunken masses scattered across them in the fall and spring. The oyster bars located next to mussel bars located next to crab shacks.

Everything about alcohol in the city evoked a unique joy. Joy in knowing that, unlike in DC, talking about where you work makes you less interesting, not more. Joy in knowing that you don't need a headline act in town to have a great time. This brand of joy is unfortunately experienced by a privileged few like me, but that's a different essay.

For all the nostalgia that comes from reflecting on city living in my early twenties, drinking with friends wasn't what made Baltimore so special. Not even close. After all, there's beer here in Boulder. Better beer. What I begin to miss most about Baltimore are the little things I know I'll never experience here, some of which I fear I'll never experience again.

First off, I miss Snowballs. Those reading this from Baltimore are probably thinking "of course!" while those unfamiliar with Snowballs are thinking "why would you miss shaved ice?"

The answer is simple: The texture of a Snowball is the texture of heaven's clouds, and the flavor is that of childhood. When I lived in Timonium for a summer, I ate a Snowball from a yellow and blue shack on Falls Road every day that it didn't rain. When I lived downtown, I ventured along Eastern Avenue every week for one.

I always ordered the same thing, kind of. I'd go "Yeah, umm, I'll do a large, and let's go half coconut half uhhhh . . . (at this point, I'd gaze across the gallery of technicolored flavors until blurting out my second choice like there was a shot clock) . . . watermelon!"

I always got half coconut because I love the taste and because I like the way a half-white, half-brightly-colored Snowball looks. This is remarkably childish, but that's the whole point.

My love for Snowballs may have culminated in Baltimore, but it started as a kid in Chevy Chase. There was a truck named Clay Boys that would visit local pools and serve authentic Snowballs. They were so popular that the Good Humor truck would simply leave if Clay Boys pulled into the lot.

One day, I asked Mr. Clay Boy how his shaved ice was better than everywhere else in town. He responded that he was from a place outside Baltimore called Catonsville where all shaved ice was made that way. He might as well have told me he was from Candyland. Fifteen years later, I'd be living in that magic Snowball city, fulfilling this sugar-filled prophecy. I've tried some "Hawaiian Ice" in Boulder, and let's just say I'm sticking to soft serve here.

I also miss squeegee kids—young kids who stand at busy intersections throughout the city and offer to clean your windshield in exchange for a dollar. They are always Black, which matters because squeegee kids are one of the most contentious subjects in the city. At dinner tables, barstools, and city hall alike, debates rage over what to do about these Black kids living in poverty, working for money.

Supporters see entrepreneurs turning to honest work on the streets. Critics see thugs; extortionists shaking honest, usually white citizens from their hard-earned money. My girlfriend saw her students. I saw kids having fun, ribbing each other over who raked in more money.

Was it uncomfortable when I pulled up next to a squeegee kid without cash? Yes, especially when they washed my window anyway, but that says more about me than it does about them. Sometimes cops were stationed at corners where squeegee kids congregated. This was supposedly to prevent crime, which happened occasionally in reality and in perpetuity on the local news.

But it was really to make commuters like me feel comfortable. "Nice. This eight-year-old can't rip me from my car and drive off—there's a cop here!"

This comfort is stolen from those kids and transferred to me, as the police do not evoke feelings of peace in their communities. Apparently, squeegee kids were prevalent in New York throughout the nineties before then mayor, and now Trump-sidekick and buffoon, Rudy Giuliani "cleaned up the streets."

I hope that never happens in Baltimore. Squeegee kids are Baltimore's sign that there's soul here, no matter how hard you try to look away. Boulder is a city that will never be described as having soul, and that's fine. But I'm not paying $25 to wash my car here, and my windshield is quite dirty.

I miss the streets. The narrow, uneven, weeds-sprouting-from-the-concrete streets. Baltimore tourism likes to showcase the historic, cobblestone lanes of Fells Point, primarily Thames Street.

It's beautiful, and on a clear fall night—when the moon reflects off the water, streetlamps illuminate the leaves and the stones, and the shoppers harmonize with the barflies—it can feel like you've traveled back to 1870. Simpler times, supposedly.

One week, when I was living on Cambridge Street between Fells Point and Canton, they tore up the street and the sidewalks to repave the road. This meant no parking for five days. The fastest way to start a war in Canton is to interfere with residents' parking. But then something amazing happened.

For two days, the cobblestone foundation of our street was exposed. The stones on Cambridge Street were laid out identically to those on Thames Street. I walked the length of the exposed block. Then I stood in the middle for ten minutes, lost in the moment. I imagined horse-drawn carriages trotting by; newsboys shouting the latest proclamation from President Grant or the incorporation of Standard Oil.

Without success, I tried to smell fresh fish caught from the harbor along Boston Street just two hundred yards away. I wondered what buildings were standing then and which ones sprouted later.

My house was built in 1860, a year before the start of the Civil War. The luxury townhomes at the water's edge certainly weren't here then. Those went up in 2010, two years after the election of our first African American president.

What struck me was how this amazing rush of history, this sense that this place matters, and that someone might one day imagine my steps here, happened on previously insignificant Cambridge Street, a place you won't see on souvenir maps.

It's the street that runs behind the Sip & Bite diner, one of the city's restaurants featured on Guy Fieri's *Diners, Drive-Ins, and Dives*. Everywhere I looked there was history. I was proud to call Baltimore home.

I miss lacrosse, a sport played in other cities. I won't say that to Baltimore natives though. To locals, their city is the epicenter of the sport, and whatever high school they went to is the best at it.

Step inside a Baltimore sports bar on a spring Saturday and you'll find three things: a college lacrosse game on TV, a local kid playing in that game, and a patron who claims to personally know that player.

Since *Inside Lacrosse* began ranking high school teams every season, I don't think one year has passed without two Baltimore-area schools making the top ten. This success justifies an exuberance of pride, which can (and does) lead to arrogance, which—when paired with affluence, also prevalent in the sport—can get ugly.

That ugliness has manifested itself into many shameful episodes of racism and unchecked privilege. But this ugliness is not the sport itself, and I miss it. It was invented by the Iroquois and is a masterful combination of brutality and grace.

Sometimes it plays like performance art; a touring exhibition of skill where players handle their sticks so naturally, you'd think it's part of their body. Sometimes it plays like a nineteenth-century football poster, with a cloud of dirt concealing all but five arms, two heads, and one broken leg as players fight for a loose ball—a thrill to watch.

I'm not supposed to miss Baltimore, even if it's natural to miss home after moving. Everyone told me I was going to love Boulder. That it was paradise, and in many ways it is. The entire state of Coloado had 293 homicides in 2020. Baltimore racked up 335 and has averaged more than three hundred a year for decades.

Boulder has idyllic weather and backyard trails that would pass as national parks in Maryland. Baltimore has winters where fire hydrants explode and a harbor that's toxic to swim in.

Yet here I am, in the greatest city to live in according to national publications, and all I can think about are the things I miss in Baltimore: the Camden Yards ballpark and crab cakes; pink and yellow pens from Big Boyz Bail Bonds. Or Barry Glazer, the medical malpractice lawyer with commercials so absurd they deserve study in film schools around the world.

Or the Canton Ping Pong Club at O'Donnell's Pub, where my Blazing Paddles went 5–25 over three seasons. Or the way people print the Maryland flag onto—and I cannot stress this enough—everything.

I wish I had the answer to what makes the city so unforgettable. Sometimes I think it's the underdog status. When the forty-fifth president of the United States spat on Baltimore via Twitter, Baltimore spat right back, harder.

Other times I think it's the optimism. Sometimes I try convincing myself I'm wrong. That the place is forgettable and I'm just some privileged sap who spent his immediate postgrad years in the safest, richest parts of the city.

But I've met too many people from all walks of life who adore Baltimore for different reasons than I do for that to be true. Maybe the answer takes a lifetime to arrive. It comes to you amidst your dying breath. That would be fitting. Good news about Baltimore never makes the headlines anyway.

The Baltimore Waterfront, 1981. Credit: Allen Baker.

Contributors

Gary M. Almeter is a writer and attorney who lives in Baltimore with his wife, three children, and two dogs. He published his first book, a memoir/biography hybrid called *The Emperor of Ice-Cream*, in 2019. His first novel, *Kissing the Roadkill Back to Life*, will be published in June 2022, and his humor book, *The Official Dream Dinner Party Handbook*, is slated for publication in July 2022.

Bradley Alston is a board member of the Baltimore Blues Society and regularly writes features for the society's newsletter, *Blues Rag*.

Rafael Alvarez is a writer based in his hometown of Baltimore, the setting for virtually all of his fiction, journalism, and memoir. His biography of a Baltimore badass turned do-gooder—*Don't Count Me Out: The Bruce White Story*—will be released in 2022 by Cornell University Press. A former staff writer for the HBO drama *The Wire*, Alvarez learned his craft on the city desk of the *Baltimore Sun* as a young man. He can be reached at orlo.leini@gmail.com.

Julia Beavers is a lifelong Baltimorean with deep roots on the city line in Dundalk. She tells stories of life, love, and Prudence Farrow while serving the best pizza in Baltimore at Matthew's in Highlandtown.

Jennifer Bishop, a graduate of Johns Hopkins University, was the original photographer for the Baltimore *City Paper* when the alternative debuted in 1977. Her work is among the most recognized in the city.

Reese Cassard is a copywriter living in Boulder, Colorado. Last year, he hit three home runs in one season of coed softball. He also got married.

Ron Cassie is a senior editor at *Baltimore* magazine, where his work has won several national awards and has appeared in partnership with the Pulitzer Center. His first book, *If You Love Baltimore, It Will Love You Back*, was published by Apprentice House in 2020. Prior to becoming a writer, he swung a hammer, poured drinks, and pedaled a bike to earn a living.

Andrée Rose Catalfamo, a writer and professor, is currently teaching rhetoric and composition at SUNY Cortland while working on two projects: a memoir, and a novel about life in 1960s Baltimore. A Baltimore native, Andrée misses Orioles baseball, crab cakes, and the Visionary Art Museum, as well as her family and friends. Andrée lives happily with her husband, the poet Burt Myers, in Binghamton, New York.

Tara Coxson Crawley is an educator in Baltimore City Public Schools.

Doug Donovan was an investigative reporter at the *Baltimore Sun* for a dozen years over two stints, both of which involved takedowns of mayors. He was part of the 2020 Pulitzer Prize-winning team that forced the resignation and criminal conviction of Mayor Catherine Pugh and promoted the overhaul of the University of Maryland Medical System's board of directors. The married father of three now works in communications at Johns Hopkins University, where he has managed digital content for the school's coronavirus website. He is also working on finishing a novel, a screenplay, and a TV pilot. He has performed in multiple storytelling and comedy shows, and his acting work includes a heart-wrenching turn as the avenging son in the ID Channel's *Evil Kin: Never Forgive, Never Forget* (season 4, episode 9) and as a reporter named Doug Donovan in the "documentary-ish" film *2030* (available on Amazon).

William Duppins is a Baltimorean currently training for work in the solar panel industry. This is his first published work.

Scot Ehrhardt published his first collection of poetry, *One of Us Is Real*, in 2016. His work has appeared in *Little Patuxent Review, Tidal Basin Review,* and *Lines + Stars*. His current project is an ergodic hybrid of poetry and escape room, which he may never finish.

David Michael Ettlin spent forty years as a City Desk editor and rewrite man at the *Baltimore Sun*. When a foreign correspondent on deadline got Ettlin on the phone, they breathed a sigh of relief—it was going to go well.

Kondwani Fidel is the author of *The Antiracist, Hummingbirds in the Trenches,* and *Raw Wounds*. He received his MFA in creative writing and publishing arts from the University of Baltimore. NPR has called Fidel "one of the nation's smartest young Black voices."

Bruce Goldfarb is the author of *18 Tiny Deaths: The Untold Story of the Woman Who Invented Modern Forensics.*

Jerome Gray is an architect and artist based in Baltimore. He founded Jerome C. Gray Architect, LLC in 2013, and since 2014, he has undertaken documenting the history of architects, buildings, and sites through exhibitions, lectures, and a daily social media feed that includes field sketches and descriptions of the city's neighborhoods. He was born in Detroit.

Jen Grow's work has appeared in the *Writer's Chronicle, About Place Journal,* the *Sun Magazine,* the *GSU Review, Hunger Mountain, Indiana Review,* and many others. Her debut story collection, *My Life as a Mermaid,* won the Dzanc Books Story Collection Competition, and she was awarded the 2016 Mary Sawyers Baker Prize, a Ruby Award from the Robert W. Deutsch Foundation, and two Individual Artist Awards from the Maryland State Arts Council. She lives in Baltimore and can be reached at www.jengrow.com.

Dean Krimmel is a museum consultant, public historian, and unrepentant Baltimore navel-gazer. He has spent the past forty years documenting through exhibitions and tours all things Baltimore—from public markets, Black churches, and department stores to the history of immigration, rowhouses, a-rabbing, and Christmas gardens. He grew up in Northwest Baltimore.

Doug Lambdin teaches at Mount St. Joseph High School. He loves all things Baltimore, especially its crab cakes and lacrosse. But sauerkraut for Thanksgiving? No—every man has his limits.

Lawrence Lanahan is the author of the narrative nonfiction book *The Lines Between Us: Two Families and a Quest to Cross Baltimore's Racial Divide.* A journalist, radio producer, and musician, he lives in the Hamilton neighborhood of Northeast Baltimore with his wife and two children and performs with his band, Disappearing Ink.

Dan Maloney, formerly of Baltimore, teaches high school English in a Philadelphia suburb. When not writing, he embroiders and prepares meals from the Barefoot Contessa cookbook.

Christopher McNally is an attorney with a deep love for all things Baltimore, particularly the history of the city's long-gone trolley car system.

Ashley Minner is a community-based visual artist from Baltimore and an enrolled member of the Lumbee Tribe of North Carolina. She earned her MFA (2011) and MA (2007) in community arts from the Maryland Institute College of Art and her PhD (2020) in American Studies from the University of the Maryland College Park. She especially enjoys spending time with her family, listening to old music, and traveling.

Jackie Oldham, a Baltimore native, is a poet and essayist. Her poems have appeared in *Oddball Magazine* and *Global Poemic*. She blogs about all things Baltimore at baltimoreblackwoman.com and is a cofounder and contributor to braciolejournal.com.

Claimed by several cities along the Eastern Seaboard, **Edgar Allan Poe** (1809–1849) won his first story contest—and $50—with a tale penned in Baltimore: "MS. Found in a Bottle." His fame and influence cannot be understated. He is buried at the corner of East Fayette and Greene Streets, where each New Year's Eve, Rafael Alvarez and Tyrone Crawley host an early morning reading of his work.

Fernando Quijano III is the Word Pimp. His fiction, nonfiction, and poetry have appeared in numerous publications, including *Hopkins Review*. He was awarded a "B Grant" from the William G. Baker Jr. Memorial Fund. You can find his work on his blog: *The Word Pimp Spits Wisdom Like Seeds.*

Mike Ricigliano—known as Ricig—is a freelance cartoonist whose sports cartoons have appeared in newspapers across the country. He began as a writer/artist for *Cracked* magazine and is beloved in Baltimore for creating a papier-mâché dummy of former Baltimore Colts owner Robert Irsay, which found its way into many saloon lavatories in and around Crabtown, USA.

Ralph Sapia is an attorney practicing family law in Baltimore. His family owned several restaurants in Ocean City, Maryland, during his childhood and early adulthood.

John Sarbanes represents the Third Congressional District of Maryland in the US House of Representatives.

Rosalia Scalia is the author of the short story collection *Stumbling toward Grace*, published in 2021 by Unsolicited Press of Portland, Oregon. She is a lifelong resident of Baltimore's Little Italy.

Len Shindel is a poet, retired steelworker, and a lifelong union man. He lives in Garrett County, Maryland, and Baltimore.

Dean Bartoli Smith is a poet with deep roots in Baltimore, tracing his family back to the Orangeville and Govans neighborhoods. His most recent book of verse is *Baltimore Son* from Stillhouse Press of Northern Virginia.

Seth Sawyers's essays and stories have appeared in *River Teeth*, *Southeast Review*, the *Baltimore Sun*, *Sports Illustrated*, *Literary Hub*, *Salon*, and elsewhere. Originally from Rawlings, Maryland, near Cumberland, he lives in Remington with his wife, the artist Magan Ruthke. He misses a lot of things and has lived in Baltimore long enough to miss more than one bar, among them Friends, Wharf Rat, and now, the Dizz.

Jean Thompson is a volunteer with the Maryland Women's Heritage Center, where she researches the roles of Maryland women in the suffrage movement.

M. Dion Thompson, known to some as "Delta Dion," is an Episcopal priest in the Diocese of Maryland. Before taking up the clerical collar, he had a twenty-year career as a newspaper reporter. He and his wife, Jean, have one son, Tevin.

Charlie Vascellaro, the author of a biography of Hall of Fame slugger Hank Aaron, is a frequent speaker on the academic baseball conference circuit. His articles on the national pastime have appeared widely, including in the *Washington Post*, the *Baltimore Sun* and the *Los Angeles Times*.

Lynne Viti, a native Baltimorean, is a former high school English teacher and a lecturer emerita at Wellesley College. She is the author of *Dancing at Lake Montebello* (Apprentice House Press), *Baltimore Girls*, and *The Glamorganshire Bible*, as well as a short fiction collection, *Going Too Fast* (Finishing Line Press). Currently living in the Boston area, she blogs at lynneviti.wordpress.com.

D. Watkins is editor at large for *Salon*. His work has been published in the *New York Times*, the *Guardian*, and *Rolling Stone* among many others. He holds a master's in education from Johns Hopkins University and an MFA in creative writing from the University of Baltimore.

Afaa Weaver came of age in working-class East Baltimore in the early days of integration and has vivid memories of the changing city. A former Fulbright Fellow, he won the Kingsley Tufts Poetry Award in 2014.

Ron Kipling Williams is a Rock 'n' Roll Buddha, a twenty-first-century Jedi, a mind-traveling, duality-processing professor whose mission is to break down walls, engage in open and honest conversations, and build community. He does this through the practice of writing, theater, and spoken word. Ron has performed in numerous theaters, universities, community centers, festivals, and in many unexpected spaces, and he blogs on a weekly basis at www.ronkiplingwilliams.com.

Helen Yuen supports Baltimore's vibrant arts and cultural life, having worked at institutions such as Creative Alliance, the American Visionary Art Museum, and the Lewis Museum of Maryland African American History and Culture. She also joins in music jams around town, public art projects, and other chances to be an active part of Baltimore's many communities.

Michael Ziegler grew up in the Northeast Baltimore neighborhood of Belair-Edison in the 1960s. He now lives in Monkton, Maryland, with his lifelong sweetheart Maud and their two cats. Mike and Maud's two daughters and grandchildren—along with summers spent in Ocean City, Maryland—make life all it can possibly be.